REQUIEM
FOR THE
AMERICAN
DREAM

REQUIEM FOR THE AMERICAN DREAM

THE 10 PRINCIPLES OF CONCENTRATION OF WEALTH & POWER

NOAM CHOMSKY

Based on the film *Requiem for the American Dream*

CREATED AND EDITED BY
PETER HUTCHISON, KELLY NYKS & JARED P. SCOTT

SEVEN STORIES PRESS
New York • Oakland • London

SEVEN STORIES PRESS
140 Watts Street
New York, NY 10013
www.sevenstories.com

College professors may order examination copies
of Seven Stories Press titles for free.
To order, visit www.sevenstories.com/textbook
or send a fax on school letterhead to (212) 226-1411.

Library of Congress Cataloging-in-Publication Control Number
2016054121

Printed in the United States

9 8 7 6 5 4 3 2 1

Table of Contents

A Note on the American Dream

DURING THE Great Depression, which I'm old enough to remember, it was bad—much worse subjectively than today. But there was a sense that we'll get out of this somehow, an expectation that things were going to get better, "maybe we don't have jobs today, but they'll be coming back tomorrow, and we can work together to create a brighter future." This was a time of a lot of political radicalism that would hopefully lead to a different future—one with more justice, equality, freedom, breaking down repressive class structures, and so on. There was just a general sense that "this will work out somehow."

Most of my family, for instance, were unemployed working class. The rise of the union movement itself was a reflection of, and a source of, optimism and hopefulness. And that's missing today. Today, there's a general feeling that nothing's coming back—*it's over.*

The American Dream, like most dreams, has large elements of myth to it. Part of the nineteenth-century dream was the Horatio Alger story—"we're dirt-poor but we're going to work hard and we'll find a way out," which was true to an extent. Take my father, he came in 1913 from a very poor village in eastern Europe. He was able to get a job in a sweatshop in Baltimore, and gradually work himself up to the point where he could go to college, get a degree, and finally even a PhD. He ended up living what's called a "middle-class" lifestyle. A lot of people could do that. It was possible for immigrants from Europe, in the early days, to achieve a level of wealth, privilege, freedom, and independence that wouldn't have been imaginable in their countries of origin.

By now we simply know that that's not true anymore. Social mobility, in fact, is lower here than it is in Europe. But the dream persists, fostered by propaganda. You hear it in every political speech, "vote for me, we'll get the dream back." They all reiterate it in similar words—you even hear it from people who are destroying the dream, whether they know it or not. But the "dream" has to be sustained, otherwise how are you going to get people in the richest, most powerful country in world history, with extraordinary advantages, to face the reality that they see around them?

Inequality is really unprecedented. If you look at total inequality today, it's like the worst periods of American history. But if you refine it more closely, the inequality comes from the extreme wealth in a tiny sector of the population, a fraction of 1 percent.

There were periods like the Gilded Age in the 1890s and the Roaring Twenties and so on, when a situation developed rather similar to this, but the current period is extreme. Because if you look at the wealth distribution, the inequality mostly comes from super-wealth—literally, the top one-tenth of a percent are just *super-wealthy*. This is the result of over thirty years of a shift in social and economic policy. If you check you find that over the course of these years the government policy has been modified completely against the will of the population to provide enormous benefits to the very rich. And for most of the population, the majority, real incomes have almost stagnated for over thirty years. The middle class in that sense, that unique American sense, is under severe attack.

A significant part of the American Dream is class mobility: You're born poor, you work hard, you get rich. The idea that it is possible for everyone to get a decent job, buy a home, get a car, have their children go to school . . .

It's all collapsed.

Introduction

TAKE A look at American society. Imagine yourself looking down from Mars. What do you see?

In the United States, there are professed values like democracy. In a democracy, public opinion is going to have some influence on policy, and then the government carries out actions determined by the population. That's what democracy means.

It's important to understand that privileged and powerful sectors have never liked democracy and for very good reasons. Democracy puts power into the hands of the general population and takes it away from the privileged and the powerful. It's a principle of concentration of wealth and power.

THE VICIOUS CYCLE

Concentration of wealth yields concentration of power, particularly so as the cost of elections skyrockets, which forces the political parties even more deeply into the pockets of major corporations. This political power quickly translates into legislation that increases the concentration of wealth. So fiscal policy, like tax policy, deregulation, rules of corporate governance, and a whole variety of measures—political measures designed to increase the concentration of wealth and power—yields more political power to do the same thing. And that's what we've been seeing. So we have this kind of "vicious cycle" in progress.

THE VILE MAXIM

I mean, the wealthy always did have an inordinate amount of control over policy. Actually, that goes back centuries. It is so traditional that it was described by Adam Smith in 1776. You read the famous *Wealth of Nations*. He says, in England, "the principal architects of policy" are the people who own the society—in his day, "merchants and manufacturers." And they make sure that their own interests are very well cared for, however "grievous" the impact on the people of England, or others. Now it's not merchants and manufacturers, it's financial institutions and multinational corporations. The people who Adam Smith called the "masters of mankind"—and they're following "the vile maxim," "All for ourselves and nothing for anyone else." They're just going to pursue policies that benefit them and harm everyone else.

Well, that's a pretty general maxim of politics that's been studied closely in the United States. Those are the policies that have increasingly been followed, and in the absence of a general popular reaction, that's pretty much what you'd expect.

PRINCIPLE #1
REDUCE DEMOCRACY

RIGHT THROUGH American history, there's been an ongoing clash between pressure for more freedom and democracy coming from below, and efforts at elite control and domination coming from above. It goes back to the founding of the country.

THE MINORITY OF THE OPULENT

James Madison, the main framer of the Constitution, who was as much of a believer in democracy as almost anybody in the world in that day, nevertheless felt that the United States system should be designed, and indeed with his initiative was designed, so that power rests in the hands of the wealthy. Because the wealthy are the more responsible set of men, those who have the public interest at heart, not just parochial interests.

Therefore, the structure of the formal constitutional system placed most power in the hands of the Senate.

Remember, the Senate was not elected in those days. In fact, not until about a century ago. It was picked by legislatures and had long terms and was selected from the wealthy. More responsible men. Men who, as Madison put it, had sympathy for property owners and their rights. And that has to be protected.

The Senate had most of the power, but it also was the most remote from the population. The House of Representatives—which was closer to the population—had a much weaker role. The executive—the president—was more of an administrator in those days, with some responsibility for foreign policy and other matters. Quite unlike today.

A major question was to what extent should we permit real democracy? Madison discussed this pretty seriously, not so much in the Federalist Papers—which were kind of propaganda—but in the debates of the Constitutional Convention, which are the most interesting place to look. If you read the debates, Madison said the major concern of the society—any decent society—has to be to "protect the minority of the opulent against the majority." His phrase. And he had arguments.

See *Secret Proceedings and Debates of the Convention Assembled at Philadelphia, in the Year 1787* on page 9

Madison observed that the model he had in mind—England of course—was the most advanced country and political society of the day. He said, suppose in England everyone had a vote freely. Well, the majority of the poor would get together and they would organize to take away the property of the rich. They would carry out what today we would call land reform: break up the big estates, break up agricultural states and give people their own land, take the land from which not long ago they had been driven by the enclosure system. So they'd vote to take over what had been the commons before and take it for themselves.

And, Madison said, that would obviously be unjust, so you can't have that. Therefore, the constitutional system has to be set up to prevent democracy—the "tyranny of the majority" it was sometimes called—to insure that property of the opulent is not interfered with.

So that's the structure of the system, it was designed to prevent the danger of democracy. Of course, in Madison's defense we should say that he was precapitalist. He assumed that the wealth of the nation would be kind of like Roman gentlemen of the mythology of the day—enlightened aristocrats, benign figures working and dedicating themselves to the welfare of all, and so on. That was one view, and it was a pretty standard one as you can see from the fact that Madison's constitutional system was in fact installed.

And I should say that, by the time you get to the 1790s, Madison was bitterly condemning the deterioration of the system he'd created, with stockjobbers and other speculators taking over, destroying the system in the name of their own interests, and so on.

ARISTOCRATS AND DEMOCRATS

There was another picture—in words at least, and partly in belief—expressed by Jefferson, the leading democratic theorist. Not so much in his own actions, but in his talk about them in which he made a distinction between what he called the aristocrats and the democrats. He put it pretty eloquently.

Basically, the idea of the aristocrats is that power has to be vested in a special class of particularly distinguished and privileged people, who will make the decisions and do the right thing. The democrats believed that power should be in the hands of the population. Ultimately, they are the repository of decision making and also ultimately of sensible action, but whether we like their decisions or not, that's what we should be supporting. He was supporting the democrats, not the aristocrats. That's kind of the opposite of the Madisonian view, though, as I said, it didn't take long for Madison to see where the system was going—and that schism runs right through American history to the present moment.

See "Thomas Jefferson in a letter to William Short," January 8, 1825, on page 10

REDUCE INEQUALITY

It's of some interest that this debate has a hoary tradition. It goes back to the first work on political democracy in classical Greece. The first major book on political systems is Aristotle's *Politics*—a long study that investigates many different kinds of political systems. He concludes that of all of them, the best is democracy. But then he points out exactly the flaw that Madison pointed out. He wasn't thinking of a country, he was thinking of the city-state of Athens, and remember, his democracy was for free men.

See Aristotle's *Politics*, ook III, Chapter 8, on page 11

But the same was true for Madison—it was free men, no women—and of course not slaves.

Aristotle observed the same thing that Madison did much later. If Athens were a democracy for free men, the poor would get together and take away the property of the rich. Well, same dilemma, but they had opposite solutions. Madison's solution was to *reduce democracy*—that is, to organize the system so that power would be in the hands of the wealthy, and to fragment the population in many ways so that they couldn't get together to organize to take away the power of the rich. Aristotle's solution was the opposite—he proposed what we would nowadays call a welfare state. He said try to *reduce inequality*—reduce inequality by public meals and other measures appropriate to the city-state. Same problem—opposite solutions. One is: reduce inequality, and you won't have this problem. The other is: reduce democracy. Well, in those conflicting aspirations you have the foundation of the country.

See Aristotle's *Politics*, Book VI, Chapter 5, on page 12

Inequality has many consequences. Not only is it extremely unjust in itself, it has highly negative consequences on society as a whole. Even on things like health. There are good studies—Richard Wilkinson and others—showing the more unequal a society is, whether it's poor or rich, the worse the health factors. Even among the rich. Because the very fact of inequality has a corrosive, harmful effect on social relations, on consciousness, on human life, and so on, which has all kinds of negative effects. Well, you know, these things ought to be overcome. Aristotle was right—the way to overcome the paradox of democracy is by reducing inequality, not reducing democracy.

THE SINS OF AMERICAN SOCIETY

There was, in the early days of the United States, an endless future of increasing wealth, freedom, achievement, and power—as long as you didn't pay too much attention to the victims. The United States was a settler-colonial society, the most brutal form of imperialism. You'd need to overlook the fact that you're getting a richer, freer life by virtue of decimating the indigenous population, the first great "original sin" of American society; and massive slavery of another segment of the society, the second great sin (we're still living with the effects of both of them); and then overlook bitterly exploited labor, overseas conquests, and so on. Just overlook those small details and then there's a certain truth to our ideals. A major question has always been, to what extent should we permit real democracy?

If you go back to the establishment of the Constitution—we're now talking about the late eighteenth century—there were conflicting views of how the new society should be organized and constructed. One crucial element that shouldn't be forgotten is the overwhelming influence of the slave states. In fact one significant factor in the American Revolution was slavery. By 1770 British justices—like Lord Mansfield, in a famous case—were already declaring slavery to be an obscenity that can't be tolerated. American slave owners could see the writing on the wall. If the colonies remained subject to British rule, pretty soon slavery would be outlawed—and there's pretty good evidence that was a major factor in the uprising, in which the slave states were very influential, Virginia being the most powerful. There were the beginnings of opposition to slavery in the Northeast, but it was small and the Constitution reflects that.

See *Somerset v. Stewart*, English Court of King's Bench, May 14, 1772, opinion delivered by Lord Mansfield, on page 12

COUNTERVAILING TENDENCIES

If you look at the history of the United States, it's a constant struggle between these two tendencies. A democratizing tendency that's mostly coming from the population, a pressure from below, which has won many victories. Women, for example—that's half the population—they did get the vote in the 1920s. (Before we feel too proud, that happens to be about the same time that women's rights were dramatically improving in Afghanistan.)

The slaves were *formally* freed, but not actually. In practice, they didn't get formal freedom until the 1960s, and even then there were many restrictions. We still have substantial residue of slavery in the contemporary system, in fact, but the property conditions on voting and participation were reduced in the nineteenth century. Then you get the beginnings of serious labor organizations—which won many victories.

So you get this constant battle going on: periods of regression, periods of progress. The 1960s, for example,

See Malcolm X's
"Democracy Is Hypocrisy"
speech, 1960, on page 13

See Martin Luther King Jr.'s
"Where Do We Go from Here?"
speech, August 16, 1967,
on page 14

See Gaylord Nelson's Earth
Day speech, April 22, 1970,
on page 15

were a period of significant democratization. Sectors of the population that were usually passive and apathetic became organized, active, started pressing their demands. And they became more and more involved in decision making, activism, and so on. It was a civilizing period—I think that's why it's called "The Time of Troubles." It just changed consciousness in a lot of ways: Minority rights. Women's rights. Concern for the environment. Opposition to aggression. Concern for other people.

These are all civilizing effects, and that caused great fear . . .

I hadn't anticipated the power—I should have—but I didn't anticipate the power of the reaction to these civilizing effects of the '60s. I didn't anticipate the strength of the reaction to it—the economic forces that would be used to deal with it, or the disciplinary techniques, the backlash.

SECRET PROCEEDINGS . . .
IN THE YEAR 1787,
AND OTHER SOURCES

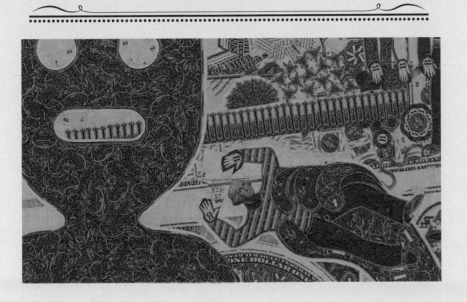

Secret Proceedings and Debates of the Convention Assembled at Philadelphia, in the Year 1787

MR. MADISON. Such are the various pursuits of this life, that, in all civilized countries, the interest of a community will be divided. There will be debtors and creditors, and an unequal possession of property, and hence arise different views and different objects in government. This, indeed, is the ground-work of aristocracy; and we find it blended in every government, both ancient and modern. Even where titles have survived property, we discover the noble beggar, haughty and assuming.

The man who is possessed of wealth, who lolls on his sofa or rolls in his carriage, cannot judge of the wants or feelings of the day laborer. The government we mean to erect is intended to last for ages. The landed interest, at present, is prevalent; but, in process of time, when we approximate to the states and kingdoms of Europe; when the number of landholders shall be comparatively small, through the various means of trade and manufactures, will not the landed interest be overbalanced in future elections, and unless wisely provided against, what will become of your government? In England, at this day, if elections were open to all classes of people, the property of the landed proprietors would be insecure. An agrarian law would soon take place. If these observations be just, our government ought to secure the permanent interests of the country against innovation. Landholders ought to have a share in the government, to support these invaluable interests, and to balance and check the other. They ought to be so constituted as to protect the minority of the opulent against the majority. The Senate, therefore, ought to be this body; and to answer these purposes, they ought to have permanency and stability. Various have been the propositions; but my opinion is, the longer they continue in office, the better will these views be answered.

Thomas Jefferson in a letter to William Short, January 8, 1825

Men, according to their constitutions, and the circumstances in which they are placed, differ honestly in opinion. Some are whigs, liberals, democrats, call them what you please; others are tories, serviles, aristocrats, etc. The latter fear the people, and wish to transfer all power to the higher classes of society. The former consider the people as the safest depository of power, in the ultimate, they cherish them therefore, and wish to leave in them all the powers to the exercise of which they are competent. This is the division of sentiment now existing in the US.

Aristotle's *Politics*, Book III, Chapter 8

The real difference between democracy and oligarchy is between poverty and wealth. Wherever the rulers, whether they be a minority or a majority, owe their power to wealth, that is an oligarchy. Wherever the poor rule, that is a democracy. Usually, where the rulers hold power by wealth, they are few, but where the poor rule, they are many, because few men are rich but all are free [if they are citizens in a city-state], and wealth and freedom are the grounds on which the two groups lay claim to government.

Democracy is not necessarily only wherever the multitude has authority. Oligarchy is not necessarily wherever a minority has power over the system of government. If the majority of a city-state were wealthy and had authority, nobody would call it a democracy, just as if a small group of poor men had control over a larger rich population, nobody would call it an oligarchy. Rather, democracy is when every free citizen has authority and oligarchy is when the rich have it.

Democracy is when there is a majority of free, poor men who have authority to rule, while oligarchy is when it is in the hands of the wealthy and well-born, who are a minority.

Aristotle's *Politics*, Book VI, Chapter 5

Poverty is the cause of the defects of democracy. That is the reason why measures should be taken to ensure a permanent level of prosperity. This is in the interest of all classes, including the prosperous themselves; and therefore the proper policy is to accumulate any surplus revenue in a fund, and then to distribute this fund in block grants to the poor. The ideal method of distribution, if a sufficient fund can be accumulated, is to make such grants sufficient for the purchase of a plot of land: failing that, they should be large enough to start men in commerce or agriculture.

Somerset v. Stewart, English Court of King's Bench, May 14, 1772, opinion delivered by Lord Mansfield

The state of slavery is of such a nature, that it is incapable of now being introduced by Courts of Justice upon mere reasoning or inferences from any principles, natural or political; it must take its rise from positive law; the origin of it can in no country or age be traced back to any other source: immemorial usage preserves the memory of positive law long after all traces of the occasion; reason, authority, and time of its introduction are lost; and in a case so odious as the condition of slaves must be taken strictly, the power claimed by this return was never in use here; no master ever was allowed here to take a slave by force to be sold abroad because he had deserted from his service, or for any other reason whatever; we cannot say the cause set forth by this return is allowed or approved of by the laws of this kingdom, therefore the black must be discharged.

Malcolm X's
"Democracy Is Hypocrisy" speech, 1960

What kind of social or political system is it when a black man has no voice in court? Has no nothing on his side other than what the white man chooses to give you? My brothers and sisters we have to put a stop to this and it will never be stopped until we stop it ourselves. They attack the victim and then the criminal who attacked the victim accuses the victim of attacking him. This is American "justice." This is American "democracy" and those of you who are familiar with it know that in America democracy is hypocrisy. Now if I'm wrong put me in jail, but if you can't prove that in America democracy is not hypocrisy then don't put your hands on me. Democracy is hypocrisy. If democracy means freedom why aren't our people free? If democracy means justice why don't we have justice? If democracy means equality then why don't we have equality? Twenty million black people in this country have been like boys in the white man's house. He even calls us boys. Don't care how big you get he calls you boy. You can be a professor; to him you're just another boy.

Martin Luther King Jr.'s "Where Do We Go from Here?" speech, August 16, 1967

I want to say to you as I move to my conclusion, as we talk about "Where do we go from here," that we honestly face the fact that the movement must address itself to the question of restructuring the whole of American society. There are forty million poor people here. And one day we must ask the question, "Why are there forty million poor people in America?" And when you begin to ask that question, you are raising questions about the economic system, about a broader distribution of wealth. When you ask that question, you begin to question the capitalistic economy. And I'm simply saying that more and more, we've got to begin to ask questions about the whole society. We are called upon to help the discouraged beggars in life's marketplace. But one day we must come to see that an edifice which produces beggars needs restructuring. It means that questions must be raised. You see, my friends, when you deal with this, you begin to ask the question, "Who owns the oil?" You begin to ask the question, "Who owns the iron ore?"

Gaylord Nelson's Earth Day speech, April 22, 1970

I congratulate you, who by your presence here today demonstrate your concern and commitment to an issue that is more than just a matter of survival. How we survive is the critical question.

Earth Day is dramatic evidence of a broad new national concern that cuts across generations and ideologies. It may be symbolic of a new communication between young and old about our values and priorities.

Take advantage of this broad new agreement. Don't drop out of it. Pull together a new national coalition whose objective is to put Gross National Quality on a par with Gross National Product.

Campaign nationwide to elect an "Ecology Congress" as the 92nd Congress—a Congress that will build bridges between our citizens and between man and nature's systems, instead of building more highways and dams and new weapons systems that escalate the arms race.

Earth Day can—and it must—lend a new urgency and a new support to solving the problems that still threaten to tear the fabric of this society . . . the problems of race, of war, of poverty, of modern-day institutions.

PRINCIPLE #2
SHAPE IDEOLOGY

T HERE HAS been an enormous, concentrated, coordinated business offensive beginning in the '70s to
try to beat back the egalitarian efforts that went right
through the Nixon years.

You see it in many respects. Over on the right, you see
it in things like the famous *Powell Memorandum*—sent to
the Chamber of Commerce, the major business lobby, by
later Supreme Court justice Powell—warning them that
business is losing "control" over the society, and something has to be done to "counter" these forces.

See *Powell Memorandum*, Lewis
F. Powell Jr., 1971, on page 25

The *Powell Memorandum* said that the most persecuted
class in the United States is the capitalist class. The owners, the very rich, were totally persecuted. Everything's
been taken over by raving leftists—Herbert Marcuse,
Ralph Nader, the media, the universities—but we have
the money so we can fight back. And what we have to
do is use our economic power to save what he would call

"freedom"—meaning our power.

Of course, he puts it in terms of a defense, "defending ourselves against an outside power." But if you look at it, it's a call for business to use its control over resources to carry out a major offensive to beat back this democratizing wave.

EXCESS OF DEMOCRACY

At the liberal international end there was pretty much the same reaction. The first major report of the Trilateral Commission is concerned with this. It's called *The Crisis of Democracy*. The Trilateral Commission is liberal internationalists from the three major industrial capitalist entities—Europe, Japan, North America. The complexion of it is illustrated by the fact that the Carter administration was drawn almost completely from their ranks—so that's the opposite extreme within the political spectrum.

See *The Crisis of Democracy: Report on the Governability of Democracies to the Trilateral Commission,* 1975, on page 27

Now, they were also appalled by the democratizing tendencies of the '60s, and thought, "we have to react to it." They were concerned that there was an "excess of democracy" developing. Previously passive and obedient parts of the population—women, young people, old people, working people—what are sometimes called "the special interests"—were beginning to organize and try to enter the political arena. They said that imposes too much pressure on the system. It can't deal with all these pressures. So, therefore, they have to return to passivity and become depoliticized.

They were particularly concerned with what was happening to young people, who were in the forefront of what was happening in the '60s. The young people are getting too free and independent. The way they put it, there's a failure on the part of the schools, the universities, the churches—the institutions responsible for the "indoctrination of the young." *Their phrase*, not mine. We have to have what they called more "moderation in democracy," and then things will be fine.

The Trilateral Commission liberals went on to offer measures to reinstitute better indoctrination to control the press, drive people back into passivity and apathy, and let the "right" kind of society develop. Across this spectrum you have various proposals they've implemented, and the changes in the economy that have been orchestrated helped provide means to carry out these measures.

EDUCATION AND INDOCTRINATION

It's hard to establish direct cause/effect relationships, but it's pretty hard not to see the general tendencies. So take, say, indoctrination of the young. From the early '70s, you begin to see a number of processes under way to control college students. If you remember that time, right after the invasion of Cambodia, the country was blowing up. The colleges were closed. People were marching on Washington, and so on. And this control takes many forms. College architecture changed. New college architecture from that period (this, incidentally, is international) was consistently designed to avoid places where students can congregate. So, lead them down alleys or something, but let's not have things like Sproul Hall in Berkeley, where students can get together and do things.

Since the '70s college tuitions have started to climb, by now to ridiculous levels. Again, I don't think we have documents to show that this was specifically planned, but you can see the consequences—for one thing it deprives large parts of the population of the option of higher education. But even those who are able to go through it, most of them end up trapped by debt. If a student comes out of college with $100,000 in debt, they're trapped. There are very few options they can pursue. And the debt is structured so that they can't pay it, you can't go bankrupt, it's not like a business debt or a personal debt. It's hanging over your head for the rest of your life, they can garnish your Social Security. So you've got to devote yourself to subordination to power.

Pretty much the same thing is happening in K–12. The tendency in K–12 is reducing education to mechanical skills, and undermining creativity and independence—both on the part of teachers and students. That's what "teaching to the test" is, "No Child Left Behind," "Race to the Top." I think these should be regarded as methods of indoctrination and control. Of course, one of the other ways to do that has been to simply reduce or eliminate free education.

The rise of the charter school system is also a very thinly disguised effort to destroy the public school system. Charter schools are a way of drawing public funds into private institutions, which will undermine the public school system. You don't get better performance even with all the advantages and so on, and that's happening across the board. So destroy public institutions.

There was an article in the *New York Times* quoting some doctors who give drugs to children in impoverished areas to try to improve their performance, knowing perfectly well that there's nothing wrong with the children—there's something wrong with the society. In fact, the way they put it, we as a society have decided not to modify the society but to modify the children. These are kids coming from impoverished areas, underfunded schools, and so on. They don't do well so, therefore, we pour drugs into the children. It's not quite the case that we as a society have decided on that—the masters of the society have decided on that.

See "Attention Disorder or Not, Pills to Help in School," *New York Times*, Alan Schwarz, October 9, 2012, on page 30

CONDEMNATION OF CRITICS

This notion of being "anti-American" is quite an interesting one—it's actually a totalitarian notion—it isn't used in free societies. If someone in Italy criticized Berlusconi or the corruption of the Italian state, they're not called "anti-Italian." In fact, if they were called anti-Italian, people would collapse in laughter in the streets of Rome or Milan. In totalitarian states the notion is used. In the old Soviet Union, dissidents were called "anti-Soviet"—that was the worst condemnation. In the Brazilian military dictatorship they were called "anti-Brazilian." But these concepts only arise in a culture where the state is identified with the society, the culture, the people, and so on. So if you criticize state power—and by state I mean generally not just government but state corporate power—if you criticize concentrated power, you're against the society, you're against the people. It's quite striking that this is used in the United States, and in fact as far as I know, we are the only democratic society where the concept isn't just ridiculed. And it's a sign of elements of the elite culture that are quite ugly.

Now it's true that in just about every society, critics are maligned or mistreated. In different ways depending on the nature of the society, like maybe in the old Soviet Union in the '80s they would be imprisoned, or in El Salvador at the same time dissidents would have their brains blown out by US state-run terrorist forces. In other societies critics are just condemned, they're vilified and so on. I mean, that's normal, to be expected, and in the United States, one of the terms of abuse is "anti-American." There's an array of terms of abuse, like "Marxist," but it doesn't matter really, it's a very free society. With everything that you can criticize it remains in many ways the freest society in the world. There's repression, but among relatively privileged people, which is a big majority of the population, you have a very high degree of freedom. So if you're vilified by some commissars, who cares, you go on—you do your work anyway.

THE NATIONAL INTEREST

For Powell on the right, it's "we've got the money, we're the trustees, we'll impose discipline," and so on. For the liberals it's softer means, but we have to do the same thing. In fact the Trilateral Commission actually argued that the media are out of control, and if they continue to be so irresponsible government controls may be necessary to keep them in line. Anyone who's looked at the media knows that they were so conformist it's embarrassing. But it was too much for the liberals, on occasion doing something they didn't like.

If you look at their study, there's one interest they never mention—private business. And that makes sense—they're not a special interest, they're the national interest, kind of by definition. So, they're okay. They're allowed to have lobbyists, buy campaigns, staff the executive, make decisions—that's fine—but it's the rest, the special interests, the general population, who have to be subdued.

Well, that's the spectrum. It's the kind of ideological level of the backlash. But the major backlash, which was in parallel to this, was just redesigning the economy.

POWELL MEMORANDUM, 1971, AND OTHER SOURCES

Powell Memorandum, Lewis F. Powell Jr., 1971

DIMENSIONS OF THE ATTACK

No thoughtful person can question that the American economic system is under broad attack. This varies in scope, intensity, in the techniques employed, and in the level of visibility . . .

SOURCES OF THE ATTACK

The sources are varied and diffused. They include, not unexpectedly, the Communists, New Leftists and other revolution-

25

aries who would destroy the entire system, both political and economic. These extremists of the left are far more numerous, better financed, and increasingly are more welcomed and encouraged by other elements of society, than ever before in our history. But they remain a small minority, and are not yet the principal cause for concern.

The most disquieting voices joining the chorus of criticism come from perfectly respectable elements of society: from the college campus, the pulpit, the media, the intellectual and literary journals, the arts and sciences, and from politicians. In most of these groups the movement against the system is participated in only by minorities. Yet, these often are the most articulate, the most vocal, the most prolific in their writing and speaking . . .

TONE OF THE ATTACK

. . . Perhaps the single most effective antagonist of American business is Ralph Nader, who—thanks largely to the media—has become a legend in his own time and an idol of millions of Americans. A recent article in Fortune speaks of Nader as follows: "The passion that rules in him—and he is a passionate man—is aimed at smashing utterly the target of his hatred, which is corporate power . . ."

THE APATHY AND DEFAULT OF BUSINESS

. . . American business [is] "plainly in trouble"; the response to the wide range of critics has been ineffective, and has included appeasement; the time has come—indeed, it is long overdue—

for the wisdom, ingenuity and resources of American business to be marshalled against those who would destroy it.

RESPONSIBILITY OF BUSINESS EXECUTIVES

. . . The overriding first need is for businessmen to recognize that the ultimate issue may be survival—survival of what we call the free enterprise system, and all that this means for the strength and prosperity of America and the freedom of our people.

A MORE AGGRESSIVE ATTITUDE

It is time for American business—which has demonstrated the greatest capacity in all history to produce and to influence consumer decisions—to apply their great talents vigorously to the preservation of the system itself.

The Crisis of Democracy:
Report on the Governability of Democracies to
the Trilateral Commission, 1975

THE VITALITY AND GOVERNABILITY
OF AMERICAN DEMOCRACY

The 1960s witnessed a dramatic renewal of the democratic spirit in America. The predominant trends of that decade involved the challenging of the authority of established political, social, and economic institutions, increased popular participation in and control over those institutions, a reaction against the concentration of power in the executive branch of the federal government and in favor of the reassertion of the power of Congress and of state and local government, renewed commitment to the idea of equality on the part of intellectuals and other elites, the emergence of "public interest" lobbying groups, increased concern for the rights of and provision of opportunities for minorities and women to participate in the polity and economy, and a pervasive criticism of those who possessed or were even thought to possess excessive power or wealth. The spirit of protest, the spirit of equality, the impulse to expose and correct inequities were abroad in the land. The themes of the 1960s were those of the Jacksonian Democracy and the muckraking Progressives; they embodied ideas and beliefs which were deep in the American tradition but which usually do not command the passionate intensity of commitment that they did in the 1960s. That decade bore testimony to the vitality of the democratic idea. It was a decade of democratic surge and of the reassertion of democratic egalitarianism . . .

The 1960s also saw, of course, a marked upswing in other forms of citizen participation, in the form of marches, demonstrations, protest movements, and "cause" organizations (such as Common Cause, Nader groups, and environmental groups). The expansion of participation throughout society was reflected in the markedly higher levels of self-consciousness on the part of blacks, Indians, Chicanos, white ethnic groups, students, and women—all of whom became mobilized and organized in new ways to achieve what they considered to

be their appropriate share of the action and of the rewards
. . . Previously passive or unorganized groups in the population now embarked on concerted efforts to establish
their claims to opportunities, positions, rewards, and privileges, which they had not considered themselves entitled
to before . . .

THE DECLINE IN GOVERNMENTAL AUTHORITY

. . . The essence of the democratic surge of the 1960s was a
general challenge to existing systems of authority, public and
private. In one form or another, this challenge manifested itself in the family, the university, business, public and private
associations, politics, the governmental bureaucracy, and the
military services. People no longer felt the same compulsion
to obey those whom they had previously considered superior to themselves in age, rank, status, expertise, character,
or talents . . . Authority based on hierarchy, expertise, and
wealth all, obviously, ran counter to the democratic and egalitarian temper of the times, and during the 1960s, all three
came under heavy attack.

CONCLUSIONS: TOWARDS A DEMOCRATIC BALANCE

. . . Al Smith once remarked that "the only cure for the evils
of democracy is more democracy." Our analysis suggests
that applying that cure at the present time could well be add-
ing fuel to the flames. Instead, some of the problems of governance in the United States today stem from an excess of
democracy—an "excess of democracy" in much the same

sense in which David Donald used the term to refer to the consequences of the Jacksonian revolution which helped to precipitate the Civil War. Needed, instead, is a greater degree of moderation in democracy.

"Attention Disorder or Not, Pills to Help in School," *New York Times*, Alan Schwarz, October 9, 2012

CANTON, GA.—When Dr. Michael Anderson hears about his low-income patients struggling in elementary school, he usually gives them a taste of some powerful medicine: Adderall.

The pills boost focus and impulse control in children with attention deficit hyperactivity disorder. Although A.D.H.D. is the diagnosis Dr. Anderson makes, he calls the disorder "made up" and "an excuse" to prescribe the pills to treat what he considers the children's true ill—poor academic performance in inadequate schools.

"I don't have a whole lot of choice," said Dr. Anderson, a pediatrician for many poor families in Cherokee County, north of Atlanta. "We've decided as a society that it's too expensive to modify the kid's environment. So we have to modify the kid."

Dr. Anderson is one of the more outspoken proponents of an idea that is gaining interest among some physicians. They are prescribing stimulants to struggling students in schools starved of extra money—not to treat A.D.H.D., necessarily, but to boost their academic performance.

It is not yet clear whether Dr. Anderson is representative

of a widening trend. But some experts note that as wealthy students abuse stimulants to raise already-good grades in colleges and high schools, the medications are being used on low-income elementary school children with faltering grades and parents eager to see them succeed.

"We as a society have been unwilling to invest in very effective nonpharmaceutical interventions for these children and their families," said Dr. Ramesh Raghavan, a child mental-health services researcher at Washington University in St. Louis and an expert in prescription drug use among low-income children. "We are effectively forcing local community psychiatrists to use the only tool at their disposal, which is psychotropic medications."

REDESIGN THE ECONOMY

S INCE THE 1970s, there's been a concerted effort on the part of the "masters of mankind," the owners of the society, to shift the economy in two crucial respects. One, to increase the role of financial institutions: banks, investment firms, insurance companies, and so on. By 2007, right before the latest crash, they had literally 40 percent of corporate profits, far beyond anything in the past.

THE ROLE OF FINANCIAL INSTITUTIONS

Back in the 1950s, as for many years before, the United States economy was based largely on production. The United States was the great manufacturing center of the world. Financial institutions used to be a relatively small part of the economy and their task was to distribute unused assets like bank savings to productive activity.

That's a contribution to the economy. A regulatory system was established. Banks were regulated. The commercial and investment banks were separated, and cut back their risky investment practices that could harm private people. There had been, remember, no financial crashes during the period of New Deal regulation. By the 1970s, that changed.

Up until the early 1970s there was an international economic system, established by the victors in World War II, the United States and Britain—Harry Dexter White for the United States, and John Maynard Keynes for Britain. It was called the Bretton Woods system, and based pretty much on regulation of capital, so currencies were regulated relative to the dollar, which was linked to gold. Now, there was very little currency speculation, because

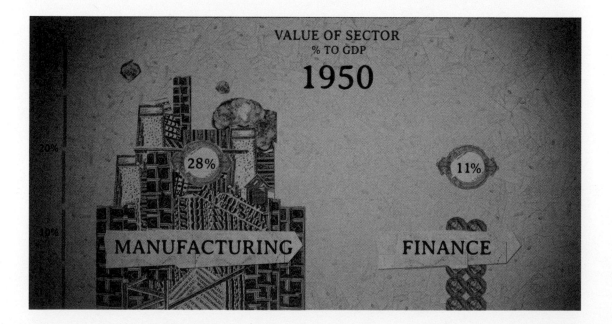

VALUE OF SECTOR
% TO GDP
1950

28%
11%

MANUFACTURING   FINANCE

there's no room for it. The International Monetary Fund was permitting, even supporting, government controls on the export of capital. The World Bank was financing state-run development projects. That was in the '50s and '60s, but by the 1970s that was dismantled. Completely dismantled. Controls on currencies were removed, which led predictably to an immediate sharp increase in speculation against currency.

FINANCIALIZATION

At the same time the rate of profit on industrial production was declining—there was still plenty of profit—but the rate was declining. So you started getting a huge increase in the flows of speculative capital—an astronomical increase—and enormous changes in the financial sec-

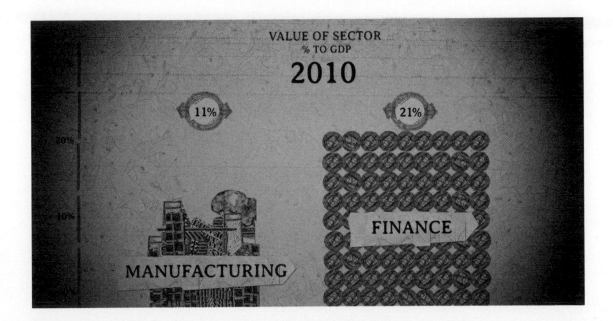

tor from traditional banks to risky investments, complex financial instruments, money manipulations, and so on.

Increasingly, the business of the country isn't production, at least not here. You can even see it in the choice of directors. The head of a major American corporation back in the '50s and '60s was very likely to be an engineer, somebody who graduated from a place like MIT, maybe industrial management. There was a sense in the ownership and management class that they'd better attend to the nature of the society—that this was their workforce, this was their market, and they had to look forward to the future of their own corporation. That's less and less true.

More recently, the directorship and the top managerial positions are people who came out of business schools, learned financial trickery of various kinds, and so on. And it's changed the attitude of the corporation and of the leadership to the firm. There's less loyalty to the firm and more loyalty to oneself. The way to get ahead now in a major firm is to show the good results in the next quarter. That's not the long-term future of the firm—it's what you can get out of the next quarter—and that also determines your salary and bonuses and so on. So if business practices can be designed to make short-term profits and you can make a ton of money and it crashes, you leave— and you've got the money and the golden parachute. That's changed the nature of the way firms are treated very significantly.

By the 1980s, say, General Electric could make more

See "An End to the Focus on Short Term Urged," *Wall Street Journal,* Justin Lahart, September 9, 2009, on page 45

profit playing games with money than it could by producing in the United States. You have to remember that General Electric is substantially a financial institution today.
It makes half its profits just by moving money around in
complicated ways. It's very unclear that they're doing anything that's of value to the economy. So what happened was
a sharp increase in the role of finance in the economy, and
a corresponding decline in domestic production. That's one
phenomenon, what's called "financialization" of the economy. Going along with that is the offshoring of production.

OFFSHORING

There's been a conscious decision to hollow out the productive capacity of the country, by shifting production to places
where there's cheaper labor, no health and safety standards,
no environmental conditions, etc.—Northern Mexico, China, Vietnam, and so on. Producers are still making plenty
of money, but they're producing elsewhere. This is all quite
profitable for multinationals—especially their managers and
executives and shareholders—but, of course, very harmful
to the population. So Apple, one of the biggest corporations, will happily produce in a Taiwanese-owned torture
chamber in China—that's about what it amounts to. China
is mainly an assembly plant. Foxconn, in Southwest China,
can produce there with parts and components sent in from
the surrounding industrial areas—Japan, Singapore, Tai-
wan, South Korea, and the United States—with the profits
coming primarily here, though there's a class of millionaires

or billionaires developing in China, too, a traditional third-world phenomenon.

In fact, what are called international "free trade agreements" are not *free* trade at all. The trade system was reconstructed with a very explicit design of putting working people in competition with one another all over the world. What it's led to is a reduction in the share of income on the part of working people. It's been striking in the United States, but it's happening worldwide. It means that an American worker's in competition with the super-exploited worker in China.

Incidentally, in China the inequality has grown enormously. China and the United States are two of the most extreme in this respect. There are plenty of labor

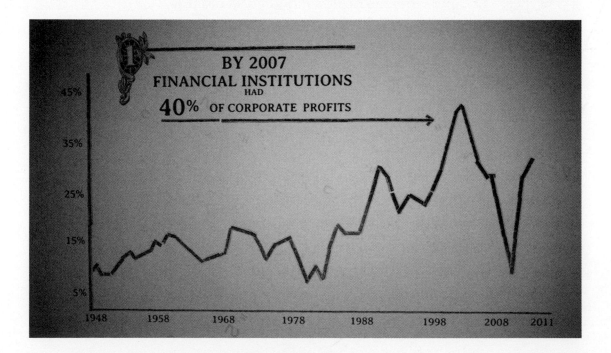

struggles in China trying to overcome this, but it's a very harsh regime. It's hard to do, but something's happening—and that's global. What the United States is exporting are operative values—the concentration of wealth, tax on working people, deprivation of rights, exploitation, and so on—that's what's being exported in the real world. It's kind of an automatic consequence of designing trade systems to protect the rich and privileged.

In the manufacturing sector in the United States, unemployment has recently been at the level of the Great Depression, but with a fundamental difference—those jobs aren't coming back, at least not under current programs. Those manufacturing jobs are not going to come back unless social policy changes. Because those who run the society, the "masters of mankind"—to once again borrow Adam Smith's phrase—they have different plans. They aren't interested in having large-scale manufacturing come back to the United States, because they can make more profit by exploiting super-cheap labor with no environmental constraints elsewhere.

Meanwhile, highly paid professionals are protected. They're not placed in competition with the rest of the world—far from it. And, of course, capital is free to move. Workers aren't free to move, labor can't move, but capital can. Again, going back to the classic authors like Adam Smith, as he pointed out, "free circulation of labor" is the foundation of any free trade system, but workers are pretty much stuck. The wealthy and the privileged are

See *An Inquiry into the Nature and Causes of the Wealth of Nations*, Adam Smith, 1776, on page 46

protected, so you get obvious consequences. And they're recognized and, in fact, praised.

WORKER INSECURITY

Policy is designed to increase insecurity. Alan Greenspan, when he testified to Congress, he explained his success in running the economy as based on what he called "greater worker insecurity." Keep workers insecure, they're going to be under control. They are not going to ask for decent wages or decent working conditions, or the opportunity of free association—meaning to unionize. If you can keep workers insecure, they're not going to ask for too much. They'll just be delighted—they won't even care if they have to have rotten jobs, they won't ask for decent wages, they won't ask for decent working conditions, they won't ask for benefits—and by some theory, that's considered a healthy economy.

The way that people in the US have been able to maintain their lifestyles in the last thirty years of stagnation is, first of all, by higher working hours. American working hours are now way beyond Europe's, benefits have declined, people are kind of getting by with debt. When you have growing worker insecurity, people go deeper and deeper into debt to try to keep going. Borrowing, buying worthless assets, inflated housing prices, all giving the illusion of wealth that you could use for consumption, for a nest egg for the future, education for your children—of course that can't go on.

The US now has much higher working hours than com-

See "Testimony of Chairman Alan Greenspan before the US Senate Committee on Banking, Housing, and Urban Affairs," February 26, 1997, on page 48

parable countries, and that has a disciplinary effect—less freedom, less time for leisure, less time for thought, more following orders, and so on—there are big effects of that. Now you see two adults in the family in the workforce, and families are collapsing because there are no public services as there are in comparable countries. If current social and economic tendencies continue, our grandchildren will increasingly be managers and executives sending jobs out to Southwest China—in these professional sectors there are going to be opportunities. But for the mass of the population it's essentially service work—you work at McDonald's.

Now, for the masters of mankind, that's fine. They make their profits. But for the population, it's devastating. These two processes, financialization and offshoring, are part of what leads to the vicious cycle of concentration of wealth and concentration of power. Producers are still making plenty of money, but they're elsewhere. The major American corporations are getting most of their profit from abroad, and that creates all sorts of opportunities to shift the burden of sustaining the society onto the rest of the population.

THE COUNTERFORCE

Now, there have been efforts to restore some form of regulatory measures, like Dodd-Frank. But the business world has lobbied very hard to create exceptions, so that much of the shadow-banking system has been exempted from regulation by lobbyist pressure. And there's gonna be constant pressure—we can be certain of it—from systems of power to prevent any constraint on expanding their power, and the profit. And the only counterforce is *you*. To the extent that the public fights back, effective systems can be created—not only to regulate the big banks, but to insist they demonstrate their legitimacy. And that challenge should be imposed on the institutions of the financial system, very broadly. That's another task for an organized, committed, dedicated population—not just to regulate them, but to ask *why they're there*.

Remember, it's not a law of nature that the United States doesn't have a manufacturing industry. Why should management make those decisions? Why shouldn't those decisions be in the hands of what are called "stakeholders," the workforce and the community? Why shouldn't *they* decide what happens to the steel industry? Why shouldn't they *run* the steel industry? These are very concrete questions. In fact, we're constantly seeing cases where, if there were enough popular mobilization and activism, we would have a productive industry manufacturing the right things. I'll mention one striking example.

After the housing bubble and the financial crash, as you remember, the government pretty much took over the auto industry. It was virtually nationalized and in government hands. That means popular hands. That meant there were choices that the public could've made. If there had been an organized, active public, there would have been choices that people like us could've made about what to do with the auto industry. Well, unfortunately, there wasn't that active mobilization and organization, so what was done was the natural thing that benefits the powerful. The industry was pretty much a taxpayer expense, and returned to essentially the same owners—some different faces, but the same banks, the same institutions, and so on—and it went on producing what it had been producing: automobiles.

There was another possibility. The industry could have been handed over to the workforce and the communities, and they could have made a democratic decision about what to do. And maybe their decision—I would at least hope that their decision—would have been to produce what the country desperately needs, which is not more cars on the street, but efficient mass transportation for our own benefit, and for the benefit of our grandchildren. If they're gonna have a world to survive in, it's not gonna be through automobiles—it's gonna be through efficient forms of transportation. Retooling it wouldn't have been that expensive, and it would be beneficial to them, beneficial to us, beneficial to the future. That was a possibility. And things like that are happening all the time, constantly.

This is one of the few countries, certainly one of the few developed societies, that doesn't have high-speed transportation. You can take a high-speed train from Beijing to Kazakhstan, but not from New York to Boston. In Boston, where I live, many people literally spend three or four hours a day just commuting. That's crazy wasted time. All of this could be overcome by a rational mass transportation system, which would also contribute significantly to solving the major problem we face—namely, environmental destruction. So that's one kind of thing that could be done, but there are many others, large and small.

So, there's no reason why production in the United States can't be for the benefit of people, of the workforce in the United States, the consumers in the United States, and the future of the world. It can be done.

"AN END TO THE FOCUS ON SHORT TERM URGED," 2009, AND OTHER SOURCES

"An End to the Focus on Short Term Urged," *Wall Street Journal*, Justin Lahart, September 9, 2009

Investors', corporate boards' and managers' focus on short-term gain has become so detrimental to the economy that unless they voluntarily change their behavior, regulators should step in, according to an Aspen Institute statement to be released Wednesday that is signed by Berkshire Hathaway Chief Executive Officer Warren Buffett, Vanguard Group founder John Bogle and former International Business Machines CEO Louis Gerstner, among others.

"We believe that short-term objectives have eroded faith in corporations continuing to be the foundation of the American free enterprise system, which has been, in turn, the foundation of our economy," said the statement, signed by 28 high-profile managers, investors, academics and others.

Over the past several decades, investors have become increasingly focused on the short term, trading more and more frequently. In 1990, for example, the average holding period of a stock trading on the New York Stock Exchange was 26 months; now it's less than nine months. At the same time, companies have become more focused on the short term as well, with managers concentrating on hitting near-term targets, such as analysts' quarterly earnings estimates, and as a result often forgoing measures that promote long-term growth, such as research and development—or even routine maintenance.

An Inquiry into the Nature and Causes of the Wealth of Nations, Adam Smith, 1776

[The] policy of Europe, by not leaving things at perfect liberty, occasions other inequalities of much greater importance.

It does this chiefly in the three following ways. First, by restraining the competition in some employments to a smaller number than would otherwise be disposed to enter into them; secondly, by increasing it in others beyond what it naturally would be; and, thirdly, by obstructing the free circulation of labour and stock, both from employment to employment and from place to place . . .

Thirdly, the policy of Europe . . . occasions in some cases a very inconvenient inequality in the whole of the advantages and disadvantages of their different employments.

The Statute of Apprenticeship obstructs the free circulation of labour from one employment to another, even in the same place. The exclusive privileges of corporations obstruct it from one place to another, even in the same employment . . .

Whatever obstructs the free circulation of labour from one employment to another obstructs that of stock likewise; the quantity of stock which can be employed in any branch of business depending very much upon that of the labour which can be employed in it. Corporation laws, however, give less obstruction to the free circulation of stock from one place to another than to that of labour. It is everywhere much easier for a wealthy merchant to obtain the privilege of trading in a town corporate, than for a poor artificer to obtain that of working in it.

The obstruction which corporation laws give to the free circulation of labour is common, I believe, to every part of Europe. That which is given to it by the Poor Laws is, so far as I know, peculiar to England. It consists in the difficulty which a poor man finds in obtaining a settlement, or even in being allowed to exercise his industry in any parish but that to which he belongs. It is the labour of artificers and manufacturers only of which the free circulation is obstructed by corporation laws. The difficulty of obtaining settlements obstructs even that of common labour. It may be worth while to give some account of the rise, progress, and present state of this disorder, the greatest perhaps of any in the police of England.

Testimony of Chairman Alan Greenspan before the US Senate Committee on Banking, Housing, and Urban Affairs, February 26, 1997

[An] acceleration in nominal labor compensation, especially its wage component, became evident over the past year. But the rate of pay increase still was markedly less than historical relationships with labor market conditions would have predicted. [A]typical restraint on compensation increases has been evident for a few years now and appears to be mainly the consequence of greater worker insecurity. In 1991, at the bottom of the recession, a survey of workers at large firms by International Survey Research Corporation indicated that 25 percent feared being laid off. In 1996 . . . the same survey organization found that 46 percent were fearful of a job layoff.

The reluctance of workers to leave their jobs to seek other employment as the labor market tightened has provided further evidence of such concern, as has the tendency toward longer labor union contracts. For many decades, contracts rarely exceeded three years. Today, one can point to five- and six-year contracts—contracts that are commonly characterized by an emphasis on job security and that involve only modest wage increases. The low level of work stoppages of recent years also attests to concern about job security.

Thus, the willingness of workers in recent years to trade off smaller increases in wages for greater job security seems to be reasonably well documented.

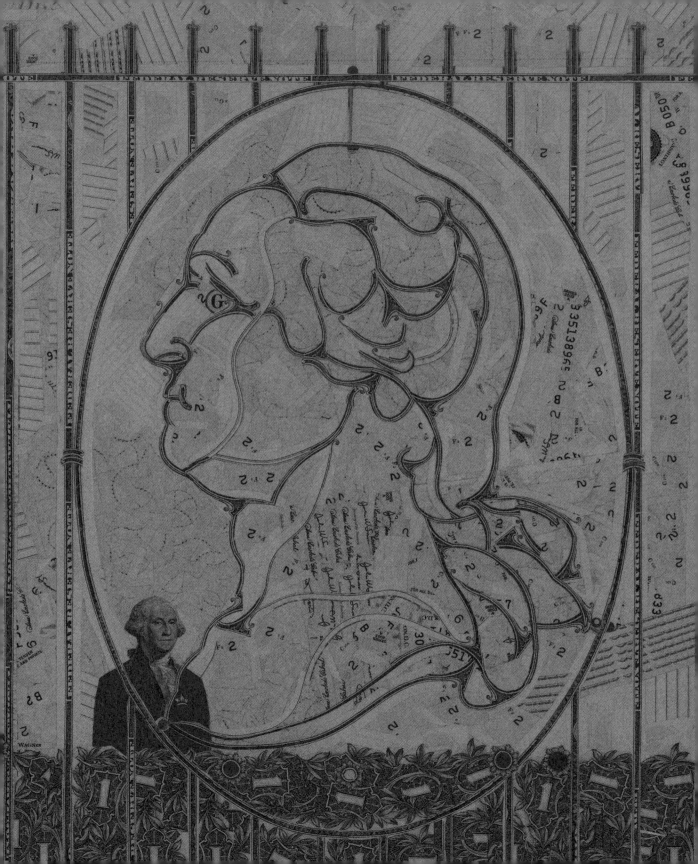

SHIFT THE BURDEN

THE AMERICAN Dream, like many ideals, was partly symbolic, but partly real. In the 1950s and '60s, say, there was the biggest growth period in American economic history. The Golden Age.

It was pretty egalitarian growth, so the lowest fifth of the population was improving about as much as the upper fifth. And there were some welfare state measures, which improved life for much of the population. It was, for example, possible for a black worker to get a decent job in an auto plant, buy a home, get a car, have his children go to school, and so on. The same was true across the board.

When the US was primarily a manufacturing center, it had to be concerned with its own consumers—here. Famously, Henry Ford raised the salary of his workers so they'd be able to buy cars.

See "Henry Ford on why he doubled the minimum wage he paid his employees" on page 59

PLUTONOMY AND PRECARIAT

Recently, there was a publication by Citigroup, one of the biggest banks. They put out a study for investors in which they identify a new category in the world—what they call the "plutonomy"—those who have substantial wealth. The plutonomy are the main drivers of the economy—they're the main consumers, that's where all the wealth goes—so Citigroup has a "plutonomy investment portfolio." They've had it since the mid-'80s, when Reagan and Thatcher in England drove forward policies of enriching the very wealthy and letting everyone else suffer. And they point out that their plutonomy investment portfolio has far outperformed the market, and urge investors to concentrate on investing for the plutonomy. So the small percentage of the world's population that's gathering together in increasing wealth—that's what you focus on. The rest you can forget about.

See *Plutonomy: Buying Luxury, Explaining Global Imbalances,* Citigroup, October 16, 2005, on page 60

When you're moving into an international plutonomy, what happens to American consumers is much less of a concern, because most of them aren't going to be consuming your products anyway, at least not on a major basis. Your goals are profit in the next quarter—even if it's based on financial manipulations—high salaries, high bonuses, produce overseas if you have to, and produce for the wealthy classes here and their counterparts abroad (mainly in the Anglosphere—the United States, Britain, Canada, and so on). And their market can be anywhere. They can sell their iPhones anywhere. So the concern for the health of the society here has substantially lessened. When the president of General Motors sixty years ago said, "What's good for GM is good for the country," that wasn't totally false. The converse was also true: "what's good for the country is good for GM." But that's much less true in the current increasingly paper economy or overseas economy.

See "From the hearings before the US Senate Committee on Armed Services when GM president Charles E. Wilson was nominated to be secretary of defense," 1953, on page 62

They've always, of course, been concerned with their salaries, but that's become their primary concern—displacing concern about the viability of the firm and, in fact, the viability of the country. It's been a tendency since the major changes that took place beginning in the late 1970s. Again, those changes are financialization—speculation, complex financial instruments, money manipulations—and offshoring, primarily.

So, it's a different attitude in general. From the point of view of the policy makers, the long-term future of the country doesn't matter so much. What matters is just those sectors of the society that sustain concentrated privilege. You have to have a powerful state to subsidize research and development, provide a cushion if you get into trouble and have to be bailed out, have a powerful military force to control the world. These are significant factors. But if, say, three quarters of the population declines into stagnation, it's much less of a concern—and, in fact, what happens to the next generation is even less of a concern.

Now, the plutonomy is much more rigorously following Adam Smith's vile maxim: "All for ourselves, nothing for anyone else." What about the rest? There's a term coming into use for them, too. They're called the "precariat," *precari-*

ous proletariat—the working people of the world who are living a more and more precarious existence. So we have the precariat living insecure, precarious lives, getting by if they can, many in terrible poverty and suffering in other ways—and the advice of Citigroup (which, by rights, the public ought to own by now, having bailed them out so often—but they're doing fine, richer than ever) is that they're asking investors to focus attention on the plutonomy. It's a really serious problem, and we're heading toward a cliff. But from the point of view of the masters of mankind, it doesn't matter much—"as long as we make plenty of profit tomorrow, who cares if our grandchildren won't have a world to live in?" It's related to the attitude toward the country altogether.

Well, that's a division the world over. In China, it's the same—it has an extremely oppressed labor force, no independent unions, tens of thousands of labor protests every year—and super-wealth. In India it's even more extreme. In other developing countries it's changing a little bit, like in Latin America. Take Brazil, a most important country, where there have been significant attempts to deal with the tremendous inequality and overwhelming problem of poverty and starvation in the past ten years. But for the most part I think the Citigroup analysis is pretty accurate—there's a plutonomy that's very rich, and the rest get by somehow if they can.

REDUCING TAXES
During the period of great growth of the economy—the '50s and the '60s but, in fact, even earlier—taxes on the wealthy

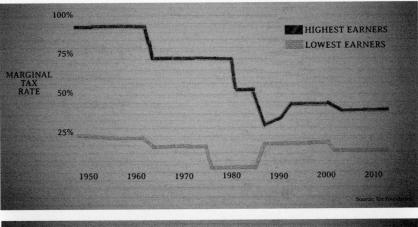

MARGINAL TAX RATE

100%

75%

50%

25%

HIGHEST EARNERS
LOWEST EARNERS

1950   1960   1970   1980   1990   2000   2010

Source: Tax Foundation

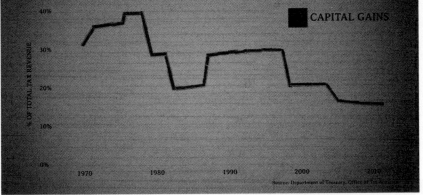

% OF TOTAL TAX REVENUE

40%

30%

20%

10%

0%

CAPITAL GAINS

1970   1980   1990   2000   2010

Source: Department of Treasury, Office of Tax Analysis

were far higher. Corporate taxes were much higher—taxes on dividends were much higher—simply taxes on wealth were much higher. Well, that's been modified, and now the shift is toward reducing taxes for those who are quite wealthy. The tax system has been redesigned so that the taxes that are paid by the very wealthy are reduced and, correspondingly, the tax burden on the rest of the population's increased. Now the shift is toward trying to keep taxes just on wages and on consumption—which everyone has to do—not, say, on dividends, which only go to the rich. And that's shifted the burden enormously. The numbers are pretty striking.

Now, there's a pretext—of course, there's always a pretext. The pretext in this case is, "well, that increases investment and increases jobs." But there isn't any evidence for that. If you want to increase jobs, if you want to increase investment, what you do is increase demand. If there's demand, investors will invest to meet it. If you want to increase investment, give money to the poor and the working people who spend it, not on expensive yachts and vacations in the Caribbean, but on goods. They have to keep alive, so they spend their incomes. That stimulates production, stimulates investment, leads to job growth, and so on.

If you're an ideologue for the masters, you have a different line. Even if there's no evidence for it, even if it makes no economic sense. In fact, right now it's almost absurd—corporations have money coming out of their pockets. It's not that they're short of money. Goldman Sachs, one of the main perpetrators of the financial crisis, is now so wealthy—thanks to government bailouts, taxpayer bailouts—that they're preparing for the next crisis. There's no shortage of cash in their hands. Pouring more cash into their hands is not in order to increase investment, or, as the term that's used, "jobs"—that's just a euphemism—it's simply in order to increase the extraordinary concentration of wealth and with it stagnation for the rest of the population. Well, that's exactly what you expect to happen when you put power in the hands of those who are going to follow the vile maxim—to maximize profit and power for themselves. "All for themselves, nothing for everyone else."

In fact, General Electric is paying zero taxes and they

See *Economic Research: How Increasing Income Inequality Is Dampening U.S. Economic Growth, and Possible Ways to Change the Tide,* Standard & Poor's, August 5, 2014, on page 62

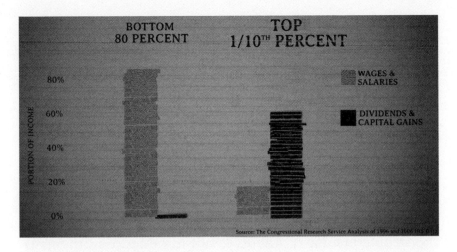

have enormous profits. This lets them take the profit somewhere else, or defer it, but not pay taxes—and this is common. The major American corporations shifted the burden
of sustaining the society onto the rest of the population.

SHIFTING IT BACK

The issue of raising taxes on the rich has, typically, been
strongly supported even by the likes of those who backed
Donald Trump in 2016—voters who pretty often have kind
of social democratic attitudes, when you look. You know,
"down with the government, but more spending on education, and health, and aid for women with dependent children." Not welfare, that was demonized—if you remember
Ronald Reagan's tales, welfare means some black man steal-
ing your money at the state office. Nobody wants that, but
you want what welfare does. People are in favor of that.

Take the 2016 Bernie Sanders campaign—across the
board, his views and positions had substantial, if not major-

ity, public support, and were pretty mainstream not long ago. The "political revolution" that Bernie Sanders called for, rightly, would not have greatly surprised Dwight Eisenhower. What that means is the spectrum has shifted so far to the right that what the population wants, and what was once mainstream, now looks radical and extremist. Well, it's up to us to shift it back. Today's Democrats are pretty much what used to be called moderate Republicans, you know, Nelson Rockefeller Republicans. That's the mainstream of the Democratic Party. The Republicans are just off the spectrum—they're not even a political party anymore.

The Republicans have moved so far toward a dedication to the wealthy and the corporate sector that they cannot hope to get votes on their actual programs, and have turned to mobilizing sectors of the population that have always been there, but not as an organized coalitional political force: evangelicals, nativists, racists, and the victims of the forms of globalization designed to set working people around the world in competition with one another while protecting the privileged. This modus operandi undermines the legal and other measures that provided working people with some protection, and with ways to influence decision making in the closely linked public and private sectors, notably with effective labor unions.

So the core question is, can that mass popular mobilization be continued and extended, and become a functioning force that'll beat back the regressive tendencies that have created a pretty ugly situation in the country?

HENRY FORD ON WHY HE DOUBLED THE MINIMUM WAGE, AND OTHER SOURCES

Henry Ford on why he doubled the minimum wage he paid his employees

"The owner, the employees, and the buying public are all one and the same, and unless an industry can so manage itself as to keep wages high and prices low it destroys itself, for otherwise it limits the number of its customers. One's own employees ought to be one's own best customers."

"It is this thought of enlarging buying power by paying high wages and selling at low prices that is behind the prosperity of this country."

Plutonomy: Buying Luxury, Explaining Global Imbalances, Citigroup, October 16, 2005

[T]he world is dividing into two blocs—the plutonomies, where economic growth is powered by and largely consumed by the wealthy few, and the rest. Plutonomies have occurred before in sixteenth century Spain, in seventeenth century Holland, the Gilded Age and the Roaring Twenties in the U.S. What are the common drivers of Plutonomy? Disruptive technology-driven productivity gains, creative financial innovation, capitalist-friendly cooperative governments, an international dimension of immigrants and overseas conquests invigorating wealth creation, the rule of law, and patenting inventions. Often these wealth waves involve great complexity, exploited best by the rich and educated of the time.

. . . We project that the plutonomies (the U.S., UK, and Canada) will likely see even more income inequality, disproportionately feeding off a further rise in the profit share in their economies, capitalist-friendly governments, more technology-driven productivity, and globalization . . .

In a plutonomy there is no such animal as "the U.S. consumer" or "the UK consumer", or indeed the "Russian consumer". There are rich consumers, few in number, but disproportionate in the gigantic slice of income and consumption they take. There are the rest, the "non-rich", the multitudinous many, but only accounting for surprisingly small bites of the national pie . . .

In addition, the emerging market entrepreneur/plutocrats (Russian oligarchs, Chinese real estate/manufacturing tycoons, Indian software moguls, Latin American oil/agriculture barons), benefiting disproportionately from globalization are logically diversifying into the asset markets of the developed plutonomies . . . Just as misery loves company, we posit that the "plutos" like to hang out together.

IS THERE A BACKLASH BUILDING?

. . . Concentration of wealth and spending in the hands of a few, probably has its limits. What might cause the elastic to snap back? . . .

A . . . threat comes from the potential social backlash . . . the invisible hand stops working. Perhaps one reason that societies allow plutonomy, is because enough of the electorate believe they have a chance of becoming a Pluto-participant. Why kill it off, if you can join it? In a sense this is the embodiment of the "American dream". But if voters feel they cannot participate, they are more likely to divide up the wealth pie, rather than aspire to being truly rich.

Could the plutonomies die because the dream is dead, because enough of society does not believe they can participate? The answer is of course yes.

. . . Our overall conclusion is that a backlash against plutonomy is probable at some point. However, that point is not now.

From the hearings before the US Senate Committee on Armed Services when GM president Charles E. Wilson was nominated to be secretary of defense, 1953

SENATOR HENDRICKSON. Well now, I am interested to know whether if a situation did arise where you had to make a decision which was extremely adverse to the interests of your stock and General Motors Corp. or any of these other companies, or extremely adverse to the company, in the interests of the United States Government, could you make that decision?

MR. WILSON. Yes, sir; I could. I cannot conceive of one because for years I thought what was good for our country was good for General Motors, and vice versa. The difference did not exist.

Economic Research: How Increasing Income nequality Is Dampening U.S. Economic Growth, and Possible Ways to Change the Tide,
Standard & Poor's, August 5, 2014

The topic of income inequality and its effects has been the subject of countless analyses stretching back generations and crossing geopolitical boundaries. Despite the tendency to speak about this issue in moral terms, the central questions are economic ones: Would the U.S. economy be better off with a narrower income gap? And, if an unequal distribution of income hinders growth, which solutions could do more harm than good, and which could make the economic pie bigger for all?

Given the decades—indeed, centuries—of debate on this subject, it comes as no surprise that the answers are complex. A degree of inequality is to be expected in any market economy. It can keep the economy functioning effectively, incentivizing investment and expansion—but too much inequality can undermine growth.

Higher levels of income inequality increase political pressures, discouraging trade, investment, and hiring. Keynes first showed that income inequality can lead affluent households (Americans included) to increase savings and decrease consumption, while those with less means increase consumer borrowing to sustain consumption . . . until those options run out. When these imbalances can no longer be sustained, we see a boom/bust cycle such as the one that culminated in the Great Recession.

Aside from the extreme economic swings, such income imbalances tend to dampen social mobility and produce a less-educated workforce that can't compete in a changing global economy. This diminishes future income prospects and potential long-term growth, becoming entrenched as political repercussions extend the problems . . .

Our review of the data, as well as a wealth of research on this matter, leads us to conclude that the current level of income inequality in the U.S. is dampening GDP growth, at a time when the world's biggest economy is struggling to recover from the Great Recession and the government is in need of funds to support an aging population.

ATTACK SOLIDARITY

SOLIDARITY IS quite dangerous. From the point of view of the masters, you're only supposed to care about yourself, not about other people. This is quite different from the people they claim are their heroes, like Adam Smith, who based his whole approach to the economy on the principle that *sympathy* is a fundamental human trait—but that has to be driven out of people's heads. You've got to be for yourself and follow the vile maxim—"don't care about others"—which is okay for the rich and powerful, but devastating for everyone else. It's taken a lot of effort to drive these basic human emotions out of people's heads.

See *The Theory of Moral Sentiments*, Adam Smith, 1759, on page 75

We see it today in policy formation—for example, in the attack on Social Security. There's a lot of talk about the crisis of Social Security, which is nonexistent. It's in quite good shape—about as good as it's ever been. Social Security is a very effective program, and has almost no administrative cost. To the extent that there's a potential crisis a couple of decades from now, there's an easy way to fix it. But policy debate concentrates on it, to a large extent, because the masters don't want it—they've always hated it, because it benefits the general public. But, actually, there's another reason for hating it.

See Social Security Act of 1935 on page 76

Social Security is based on a principle. It's based on a principle of *solidarity*. Solidarity: caring for others. Social Security means, "I pay payroll taxes so that the widow across town can get something to live on." For much of the population, that's what they survive on. It's of no use to the very rich so, therefore, there's a concerted attempt to destroy it. One of the ways is by defunding it. You want to destroy some system? First defund it. Then, it won't work. People will be angry, and they'll want something else. It's a standard technique for privatizing some system.

THE ATTACK ON PUBLIC EDUCATION

We see it in the attack on public schools. Public schools are based on the principle of solidarity. I no longer have children in school. They're grown up, but the principle of solidarity says, "I happily pay taxes so that the kid across the street can go to school." Now, that's normal human emotion. You have to *drive that out* of people's heads. "I don't have kids in school. Why should I pay taxes? Privatize it," and so on. The public education system—all the way from kindergarten to higher education—is under severe attack. That's one of the jewels of American society.

You go back to the Golden Age again, the great growth period in the '50s and '60s. A lot of that is based on free public education. One of the results of the Second World War was the GI Bill of Rights, which enabled veterans—and remember, that's a large part of the population then—to go to college. They wouldn't have been able to, otherwise. They essentially got free education. I went to college in 1945—I wasn't a veteran, I was too young, but it was virtually free. It was an Ivy League school, the University of Pennsylvania, but the tuition was one hundred dollars and you could easily get a scholarship.

See Servicemen's Readjustment Act of 1944 on page 76

I should mention that if you looked at the faces of the people who were coming out of the colleges during the period, they were all white. The GI Bill and many other social programs were actually designed on racist principles that are deeply embedded in our history, and have by no means been overcome. Nevertheless, with that aside, from the nineteenth century the US was way in the lead in developing extensive mass public education at every level.

By now, however, in more than half the states, most of the funding for the state colleges comes from tuition, not from the state. That's a radical change, and that's a terrible burden on students. It means that students, if they don't come from very wealthy families, they're going to leave college with big debts. And if you have a big debt, you're trapped. I mean, maybe you wanted to become a

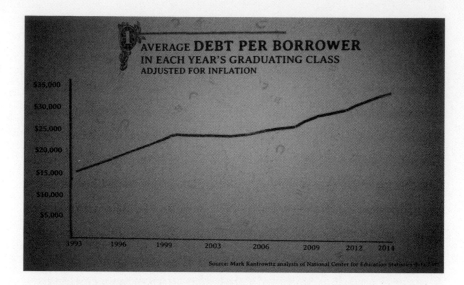

AVERAGE **DEBT PER BORROWER**
IN EACH YEAR'S GRADUATING CLASS
ADJUSTED FOR INFLATION

Source: Mark Kantrowitz analysis of National Center for Education Statistics data

public interest lawyer, but you're going to have to go into a corporate law firm to pay off those debts. And by the time you're part of the culture, you're not going to get out of it again. That's true across the board.

In the 1950s, it was a much poorer society than it is today but, nevertheless, it could easily handle essentially free mass higher education. Today, a much richer society claims it doesn't have the resources for it. That's just what's going on right before our eyes. That's the general attack on principles that—not only are they humane—are the *basis* of the prosperity and health of this society.

PRIVATIZATION

And that's constant. Take, say, some of the proposals for Medicare—basically destroying Medicare and privatizing it. They are carefully designed so that at the beginning it exempts people over fifty-five, a substantial part of the voting population. If you want to get it through the legislatures, you better get the voters. So there's a hope that the elderly will be so vicious that they're willing to punish their children and their grandchildren so that they can get decent health care. That's what the principle is based on.

And, of course, as their children grow older and grandchildren come into it, they'll be subject to the sharp cuts in medical aid that come from the design of these programs. It's designed on the "sunset principle" so that the main sector of voters will be willing to go along with it. And when the legislation's passed, then the rest—including their children and grandchildren—they'll be the ones stuck with the trillions of dollars in costs to get medical care.

We have the only health care system in the advanced world that is based overwhelmingly on virtually unregulated private health care, and that is extremely inefficient and very costly. All sorts of administrative costs, bureaucracies, surveillance, simple billing—things that just don't exist in rational health care systems. And I'm not talking about anything utopian—almost every other industrial society has them and, in fact, they are far more efficient both in outcomes and costs than the one we have in the United States. That's a scandal, but also quite apart from the millions of people who have *no insurance at all*, and are even more insecure.

I should say it's not just the insurance companies and financial institutions that are driving this but also the pharmaceutical corporations. The United States, I think, is the only country in the world in which the government, by law, is not permitted to negotiate drug prices. So the Pentagon can negotiate prices for pencils, but the government can't negotiate drug prices for Medicare and Medicaid. Actually, there's one exception to that, the Veterans Administration. They're allowed to negotiate drug prices so that they're far lower. They're at world standards. But legislation has been introduced to prevent people from benefiting from the lower prices elsewhere, of course radically in violation of free trade. The rhetoric is free trade but certainly not the policies.

In fact, the Veterans Administration is far more efficient, the drug costs are much lower, the general costs are much lower, and outcomes are better. The Medicare system itself in the United States is quite efficient, as well—administrative costs for Medicare are far below those of private insurance. And remember, these are both government health programs. Medicare costs are skyrocketing now, only because they have to work through the privatized, unregulated insurance system. It's known how to deal with these questions; in fact, we have models all around us. But you can't touch them because they're too powerful in the economy. It's kind of interesting to see what happens in the rare case when it is brought up. In the *New York Times*, occasionally it's been called "politically impossible" or "lacking political support" when, actually, a majority of the population has wanted it for a long time.

When Obama instituted the Affordable Care Act, as you may recall, there was originally talk about a public option, which means national health care. It was supported by almost two-thirds of the population. But it was dropped—no discussion. You go back even earlier to the late Reagan years, and about 70 percent of the population thought that national health care ought to be a constitutionally guaranteed right. In fact, about 40 percent of the population thought it *already* was a constitutionally guaranteed right. But that's not political support—political support means Goldman Sachs, JPMorgan Chase, and so on—that's political support. In fact, if we had a health care system like other countries, we would have no deficit, we'd probably have a surplus.

ELIMINATING GOVERNMENT

It's very striking to see the debate in the United States—also in Europe, incidentally—about the current economic problems. The major human problem, overwhelmingly, isn't the deficit—it's *joblessness*. Joblessness has a devastating effect on a society. I mean, there are terrible consequences for the people and their families. But it also has a terrible economic effect—it's pretty obvious why; when people aren't working there are resources that could develop the economy that are not being used—they're being wasted.

It sounds like an inhuman way to talk about it—the human cost is the worst part. But from a straight economic point of view, it's as if you somehow decided to leave factories idle. Take a trip to Europe, Japan, or even China, and then come back to the United States. One of the things that immediately strikes you is the country's falling apart, you often feel like you're returning to a third world country. Infrastructure has collapsed, health care is a total wreck, the educational system is being torn to shreds, nothing works, and with incredible resources. To get people to sit passively and look at that reality takes very effective propaganda. That's essentially what's happening—you have a big workforce that's eager to work, highly skilled, with lots of things that have to be done. The country needs all sorts of things.

Financial institutions don't like the idea of a deficit, and they also don't want that much of a government. This has been taken to the extreme by people like Grover Norquist, who's very influential. He has this pledge that all Republicans have to sign—and they do—which is that you're not allowed to increase taxes, that you must reduce the government. As he puts it, he wants to basically eliminate the government. Well, from the point of view of the masters, that's kind of understandable. The government does, to the extent that democracy functions, carry out actions in the interests of and determined by the population. *That's what democracy means.* And they, of course, would prefer to have total control without interference of the public. So they're happy to see the government diminished—with two caveats that have to be added. They want to make sure that there's a powerful state there that can mobilize taxpayers to bail them out and to enrich them further. And, secondly, they want a major military force to make sure that the world is under control.

That's what they want the state to be restricted to— nothing like making sure elderly people get medical care or a disabled widow gets enough to live on. That's not their business, it's not in accord with the vile maxim, so they're concentrating on the deficit. For the public, joblessness is of far greater importance. But, with few exceptions, like Paul Krugman, the public discussion remains focused on the deficit.

Overwhelmingly, the discussion is shaped by the masters: "look at the deficit, forget everything else." But even when looking at the deficit, it's very striking that they omit anything about the *causes* of the deficit. The causes of the deficit are pretty clear. One is the extraordinary military spending that's about the same as that of the rest of the world combined. Not for security, incidentally (that's another story)—it doesn't provide security except for the masters that control the world and their interests. And that's almost untouchable.

A RETURN TO SOLIDARITY

How do we make higher education more affordable? Very easy—by doing it.

Take a look at the world, at ourselves, and we see very simple answers to this. Finland comes out close to the top on virtually any measure of educational achievement—how much do you pay to go to college? *Nothing*. It's free. Take Germany, another rich country with a pretty successful educational system—how much do you pay? Essentially *nothing*. Take a poor country right near us—Mexico happens to have a pretty good higher educational system, I've been impressed with what I've seen. Salaries are very low because it's a very poor country, but how much do you pay? *Nothing*.

There is no economic reason why education can't be available to everyone for free—there are *social* and *political* reasons. But those are social and political *decisions*. In fact, the economy would almost certainly be better off if more people did have the opportunity to develop themselves and contribute to society through what higher education can offer.

THE THEORY OF MORAL SENTIMENTS, 1759, AND OTHER SOURCES

The Theory of Moral Sentiments,
Adam Smith, 1759

How selfish soever man may be supposed, there are evidently some principles in his nature, which interest him in the fortune of others, and render their happiness necessary to him, though he derives nothing from it except the pleasure of seeing it. Of this kind is pity or compassion, the emotion which we feel for the misery of others, when we either see it, or are made to conceive it in a very lively manner. That we often derive sorrow from the sorrow of others, is a matter of fact too obvious to require any instances to prove it; for this sentiment, like all the other original passions of human nature, is by no means confined to the virtuous and humane, though they perhaps may feel it with the most exquisite sensibility. The greatest ruffian, the most hardened violator of the laws of society, is not altogether without it.

Social Security Act of 1935

An act to provide for the general welfare by establishing a system of Federal old-age benefits, and by enabling the several States to make more adequate provision for aged persons, blind persons, dependent and crippled children, maternal and child welfare, public health, and the administration of their unemployment compensation laws; to establish a Social Security Board; to raise revenue; and for other purposes.

Servicemen's Readjustment Act of 1944

As used in this part, the term educational or training institutions shall include all public or private elementary, secondary, and other schools furnishing education for adults, business schools and colleges, scientific and technical institutions, colleges, vocational schools, junior colleges, teachers colleges, normal schools, professional schools, universities, and other educational institutions, and shall also include business or other establishments providing apprentice or other training on the job, including those under the supervision of an approved college or university or any State department of education, or any State apprenticeship agency or State board of vocational education, or any State apprenticeship council or the Federal Apprentice Training Service established in accordance with Public, Numbered 308, Seventy-fifth Congress, or any agency in the executive branch of the Federal Government authorized under other laws to supervise such training.

RUN THE REGULATORS

I F YOU look over the history of regulation—railroad regulation, financial regulation, and so on—you find that, quite commonly, it's either initiated by the economic concentrations that are being regulated, or it's supported by them. And the reason is because they know that, sooner or later, they can take over the regulators and essentially run what they do. They can offer what amounts to bribes—offer them jobs or whatever it may be—it's an advantage to the regulators to accommodate themselves to the will of the powerful. It happens naturally in many ways, and ends up with what's called "regulatory capture." The business being regulated is in fact running the regulators. The banks and bank lobbyists are actually writing the laws of financial regulation—it gets to that extreme. That's been happening through history and,

See *Prosperity Economics: Building an Economy for All,* Jacob S. Hacker and Nate Loewentheil, 2012, on page 91

again, it's a pretty natural tendency when you just look at the distribution of power.

GLASS-STEAGALL

During the Depression, one of the regulations instituted was to separate commercial banks, which are where deposits are federally guaranteed, from investment banks, which just take risks and there are no federal guarantees. They were separated in what was called the Glass-Steagall Act.

In the 1990s, the economic programs of the Clinton administration were run pretty much by Robert Rubin and his associates—people who basically came out of the financial industries—and they wanted to overrule this law from back in the '30s. They succeeded, in 1999, by undermining Glass-Steagall with the cooperation of right-wing Republicans, Phil Gramm and others. That meant that, essentially, the risky operations of investment banks ended up being guaranteed by the government. Well, you can see where that was going to lead—and it did. At the very same time, they also barred regulation of derivatives—exotic financial instruments—which meant that they could take off unregulated. Now all of this is quite safe as long as you know the government is going to come to your rescue.

REVOLVING DOOR

In fact, what Robert Rubin himself did after having achieved this, he went and became a director of Citigroup—one of the biggest banks—and made use of the new laws. He helped them take over a big insurance company and so on—made a lot of money—and it crashed. He went off with all his money, came back as Obama's chief adviser, and then the government bailed out Citigroup—as they've been doing for years, in fact, since the early '80s. As senators, representatives, and advisers in the government leave the government and go into the commercial industrial (by now mostly financial) systems that they've been theoretically regulating, it is almost a *consequence* to have regulatory capture. That's where their associations are, that's where they belong. So they move in and out of these systems, and what it means is that there's the same very close interaction—one aspect of which is the "revolving door." So you're a legislator and you become a lobbyist, and as a lobbyist, you want to control legislation.

LOBBYING

One of the things that expanded enormously in the 1970s as the business world moved sharply to try to control legislation is lobbying. There was a huge effort with lobbyists to try even to *write* legislation. The business world was pretty upset by the advances in public welfare in the '60s, in particular by Richard Nixon—it's not too well understood, but he was the last New Deal president, and they regarded that as class treachery.

See "How Corporate Lobbyists Conquered American Democracy," *New America Weekly,* New America, Lee Drutman, April 20, 2015, on page 92

In Nixon's administration, you get the consumer safety legislation (CPSC), safety and health regulations in the workplace (OSHA), and the EPA—the Environmental

Protection Agency. Business didn't like it, of course—they didn't like the higher taxes, didn't like the regulation. And they began a coordinated effort to try to overcome it. Lobbying sharply increased. New think tanks were developed to try to control the ideological system, like the Heritage Foundation. The spending on campaigns went way up—in part, the result of television. And there was just fantastic growth of the role of finance in the economy. With this, deregulation began with a real ferocity.

DEREGULATION AND FINANCIAL CRASHES
Remember, there were no financial crashes in the '50s and the '60s, because the regulatory apparatus of the New Deal was still in place. As it began to be dismantled

under business pressure and political pressure, you get more and more crashes, and it goes on right through the years—the '70s is where deregulation starts, and the '80s is where crashes really take off.

Take Reagan—instead of letting them pay the cost, Reagan bailed out the banks, like Continental Illinois, the biggest bailout of American history at the time, 1984. In the early 1980s, the US went into the deepest recession since the Great Depression, only to be pulled out by various forms of subsidy, and so on. In 1987, there was another financial crash—well, pretty close, Black Monday. Reagan actually ended his term with a huge financial crisis—the savings and loan crisis—and, again, the government moved in and bailed it out.

TOO BIG TO JAIL

The savings and loan crisis was a little different from the 2008 financial crisis, because the perpetrators were brought to court and tried, and a lot was learned from the trials about the chicanery, shenanigans, trickery, and crimes that were carried out. Not this last time. Power has become so concentrated that not only are the banks "too big to fail," but as one economist put it, they are also "too big to jail." The only kind of criminal investigations that can be undertaken are, for instance, insider trading, where the criminal is actually harming other businesses—that you can do something about. But where they're just robbing people, that's done with impunity.

Deregulation went on through the Clinton years. Clinton came along, and there was a tech boom—but by the end of the 1990s there was another bubble that broke, the dot-com bubble. In 1999, regulation separating commercial banks from investment banks was dismantled. Bush came along and we had the housing boom, which, amazingly, the policy economists didn't notice—or they ignored the fact that there was about an $8 trillion housing bubble that held no relation to the relevant facts about cost of housing. Of course, that broke in 2007, and trillions of dollars of capital just disappeared—fake wealth. That led to the biggest financial crisis since the Great Depression. Then comes the Bush and Obama bailout, which reconstructed the powerful institutions—the perpetrators—and left everyone else floating. There was severe harm to people, who had houses taken away from them, jobs diminished, and so on. That's where we are now. It was done with impunity, and they're building up to the next one.

THE NANNY STATE

Each time, the taxpayer is called on to bail out those who created the crisis, increasingly the major financial institutions. In a capitalist economy, you wouldn't do that. In a capitalist system, that would wipe out the investors who made risky investments. But the rich and powerful, they don't want a capitalist system. They want to be able to run to the "nanny state" as soon as they're in trouble, and get bailed out by the taxpayer. They're given a government insurance policy, which means that no matter how often you risk everything, if you get in trouble, the public will bail you out because you're too big to fail—and it's just repeating over and over again.

Their power is so enormous that any attempt to deal with it is essentially beaten back. There have been mild attempts, like the Dodd-Frank regulatory proposal, but that's whittled down in the implementation by lobbyists—and it doesn't go after the main issues anyway. And the reasons for this are pretty well understood. There are Nobel laureates in economics who significantly disagree with the course that we're following—people like Joseph Stiglitz, Paul Krugman, and others—and none of them were even approached or consulted. The people picked to fix the crisis were those who created it—the Robert Rubin crowd, the Goldman Sachs crowd. They created the crisis and are now more powerful than before. Is that an accident? Well, not when you pick those people to create an economic plan. I mean, what do you expect to happen?

The last bailout was unprecedented in scale. These corporations were kept viable in a period where, in a capitalist economy, they would've crashed. But we don't have a capitalist economy—business wouldn't accept that, and they have enough power to prevent it—so, therefore, the public comes in to pour literally trillions of dollars into the hands of failing corporations and maintain them.

And that's true in all sorts of ways. There's one major technical study of bailouts over several years that concludes that probably 25 percent—a study of the hundred biggest corporations on the *Fortune* list by two well-known economists—25 percent of them survived thanks to public subsidy at some point, and most of the rest gained from it. So while this is unprecedented in scale, there's nothing new about it. The same is true after all financial crises.

See *The Logic of International Restructuring: The Management of Dependencies in Rival Industrial Complexes,* Winfried Ruigrok and Rob van Tulder, 1995, on page 94

EXTERNALITIES AND SYSTEMIC RISK

The financial system is close to a market system—it does approximate a market, unlike the production system, which has enormous state dynamism and intervention to keep it going—and in a market system there are well-known inherent problems, namely the participants in a transaction try to take care of only themselves. They don't pay attention to the effect on others. Let's say you sell me a car. You'll try to make a profit, I'll try to get a decent car, but we're not considering the impact on others: environmental problems, congestion, rising price of fuels, and so on. Those may be individually small, but they mount up. Those are called "externalities" in economic terminology.

Now, in the case of a big investment bank like Goldman Sachs, if they make an investment or a loan, they try to calculate in the risk to themselves—of course, that's pretty easy to do when they know they're going to be bailed out because they're too big to fail. What they don't take into account is what's called "systemic risk." The risk that if their investments collapse, the whole system may collapse. Well, that's what happened, has repeatedly happened, and is probably going to happen again. And that's been exacerbated by the deregulatory mania and also by the development of very complex financial instruments, which, again, have no known contribution to the economy, but make it possible to distribute risks in complex ways.

That's what happened with the mortgage crisis. Mortgage sellers were offering subprime mortgages to people who they knew would never be able to pay them back, and the banks were picking them up as mortgage-backed securities (MBSes). But they didn't have to worry, because they did what's called "securitizing"—they broke them up into many small parts and handed them off to someone else as collateralized debt obligations (CDOs). Now, those investors often didn't even know what they were buying and, meanwhile, the instruments that allowed the buying were essentially the insurance against the failure of what you're doing. Technically that was supposed to reduce risk. What it in fact did was magnify risk in such a way that when the system suffered a break—as it did with the collapse of the housing crisis—then the effects were enormous. And again, the taxpayers were called in to bail it out. That's not just bailing out the banks, that's hundreds of billions of dollars coming out of the Fed and Treasury, providing cheap credit, and so on.

There's nothing surprising about this—it's exactly the dynamics you expect. If the population allows it to proceed, it's just going to go on and on like this. Until the next crash—which is so much expected that credit agencies, which evaluate the status of firms, are now counting into their calculations the taxpayer bailout that they expect to come after the next crash. This means that the beneficiaries of these credit ratings, like the big banks, can borrow money more cheaply, they can push out smaller competitors, and you get more and more concentration.

Everywhere you look, policies are designed this way, which should come as absolutely no surprise to anyone. That's what happens when you put power into the hands of a narrow sector of wealth, which is dedicated to increasing power for itself—just as you'd expect.

LET THE MARKET PREVAIL

The simplest definition of "neoliberalism" is "let the market run everything." Get the government out of policy formation except to support market activities. Nobody really means that. Those are measures applied to the poor and the weak but not to yourself. And that runs all through modern economic history back to the seventeenth century. They didn't call it neoliberalism then.

Take Adam Smith's recommendations to the newly liberated colonies. He was the great economist of the day, and he gave the colonies advice—which is essentially what the World Bank and IMF tell poor countries today,

See *An Inquiry into the Nature and Causes of the Wealth of Nations,* Adam Smith, 1776, on page 94

and the poor in the United States too. He said that the colonies should concentrate on what they're good at—that was later called "comparative advantage"—export primary products, like agricultural products, fish, and fur, and import superior British goods. Furthermore, don't try to monopolize your resources. The main resource in those days was cotton. That was like the fuel of the early Industrial Revolution. He pointed out to the colonies that that would improve the total economic product, and so on.

Of course, the colonies were liberated, so they were free to completely ignore "sound economics" as it was called. They imposed high tariffs to block superior British goods—at first textiles, later steel and so on—and therefore were able to develop domestic industry. They tried very hard and, in fact, almost succeeded in monopolizing cotton—that was a large part of the point of the conquest of Texas and half of Mexico. The reasons were very explicit—the Jacksonian presidents said if we can monopolize cotton, we can bring Britain to their knees. They won't be able to survive if we control the main import that they need. So, without going further into the details, the colonies did exactly the opposite of the neoliberal prescriptions (which, incidentally, Britain had also done as it developed). Meanwhile the poor and oppressed, they had these principles rammed down their throats. So India, Egypt, Ireland, and others, they were deindustrialized, deteriorated—something that continues even now.

And that's happening right in front of our eyes. Take

See "President John Tyler in a letter to his son, Colonel Tyler," April 17, 1850, on page 95

inside the United States—for the large majority of the population, the principle is you've got to "let the market prevail." Cut back entitlements, cut back or destroy Social Security, cut back or reduce the limited health care—just let the market run everything. But not for the rich. For the rich, the state is a powerful state, which is ready to move in as soon as you get into trouble and bail you out. Take Reagan, he's the icon of neoliberalism, free markets, and so on. He was the most protectionist president in postwar American history. He doubled protectionist barriers to try to protect incompetent US management from superior Japanese production. Again, he bailed out banks instead of letting them pay the costs. In fact, government actually *grew* during the Reagan years relative to the economy, and that's the icon of neoliberalism. I should add that his "Star Wars" program, SDI, was advertised openly to the business world as a government stimulus, a kind of cash cow that they could milk. But that was for the rich—meanwhile, for the poor, let market principles prevail, don't expect any help from the government, the government is the problem, not the solution, and so on. That's essentially neoliberalism. It has this dual character, which goes right back in economic history. One set of rules for the rich. Opposite set of rules for the poor.

PROSPERITY ECONOMICS, 2012, AND OTHER SOURCES

Prosperity Economics: Building an Economy for All, Jacob S. Hacker and Nate Loewentheil, 2012

As money has become more important in politics and corporate interests more organized, business groups and the affluent have gained enormous power relative to the middle class. This allows today's economic winners to create and reinforce their gains by shaping government policy, rather than by innovating in the market. These activities make the rest of Americans poorer and our political system weaker . . .

Increasingly, our political system is a two-way channel in which money flows in one direction and favorable policy flows back. Large corporations give donations, hire expensive lobbyists (often, former public officials and their staffs), and run costly faux-grassroots campaigns in pursuit of their favored policies. The revolving door in Washington swings faster and faster—between worlds that are increasingly far apart in pay and privilege. Members of Congress and their staffs and high-level executive branch officials are offered huge sums to ply their influence within the halls of power. Official expenditures on federal lobbying—which surely understate the true numbers—have risen from $460 million to over $3 billion. If business and the rich invest in the private sector for a return, they invest in politics for a return, too—only this return comes at the expense of our broader economy, taxpayers, and our democracy.

"How Corporate Lobbyists Conquered American Democracy," *New America Weekly,* New America, Lee Drutman, April 20, 2015

Something is out of balance in Washington. Corporations now spend about $2.6 billion a year on reported lobbying expenditures—more than the $2 billion we spend to fund the House ($1.18 billion) and Senate ($860 million). It's a gap that has been widening since corporate lobbying began to regularly exceed the combined House-Senate budget in the early 2000s.

Today, the biggest companies have upwards of 100 lobbyists representing them, allowing them to be everywhere, all the time. For every dollar spent on lobbying by labor unions and public-interest groups together, large corporations and their associations now spend $34. Of the 100 organizations that spend the most on lobbying, 95 consistently represent business.

One has to go back to the Gilded Age to find business in such a dominant political position in American politics. While it is true that even in the more pluralist 1950s and 1960s, political representation tilted towards the well-off, lobbying was almost balanced by today's standards. Labor unions were much more important, and the public-interest groups of the 1960s were much more significant actors. And very few companies had their own Washington lobbyists prior to the 1970s. To the extent that businesses did lobby in the 1950s and 1960s (typically through associations), they were clumsy and ineffective. "When we look at the typical lobby," concluded three leading political scientists in their 1963 study, American Business and Public Policy, "we find its opportunities to maneuver are sharply limited, its staff mediocre, and its typical problem not the influencing of Congressional votes but finding the clients and contributors to enable it to survive at all."

Things are quite different today. The evolution of business lobbying from a sparse reactive force into a ubiquitous and increasingly proactive one is among the most important transformations in American politics over the last 40 years.

The Logic of International Restructuring: The Management of Dependencies in Rival Industrial Complexes, Winfried Ruigrok and Rob van Tulder, 1995

We assess that at least twenty companies in the 1993 Fortune 100 would not have survived at all as independent companies, if they had not been saved by their respective governments. Some eighteen core firms have been nationalised, many of them during major restructuring periods, sometimes even facing immediate bankruptcy threats. The social costs for a nation as a result of the exit or demise of these core firms enabled them to demand that governments socialise their losses—albeit in return for temporary or long-term loss of autonomy. The formation of huge state-owned conglomerates such as IRI, INI (1920s–1940s) and ENI is a case in point.

An Inquiry into the Nature and Causes of the Wealth of Nations, Adam Smith, 1776

Were the Americans, either by combination or by any other sort of violence, to stop the importation of European manufactures, and, by thus giving a monopoly to such of their own countrymen as could manufacture the like goods, divert any considerable part of their capital into this employment, they would retard instead of accelerating the further increase in the value of their annual produce, and would obstruct instead of promoting the progress of their country towards real wealth and greatness. This would be still more the case were they to attempt, in the same manner, to monopolize to themselves their whole exportation trade.

President John Tyler in a letter to his son, Colonel Tyler, April 17, 1850

I have replied in a brief letter putting him right on the subject of Texas annexation. My view of that subject was not narrow, local, or bigoted. It embraced the whole country and all its interests. The monopoly of the cotton-plant was the great and important concern. That monopoly, now secured, places all other nations at our feet. An embargo of a single year would produce in Europe a greater amount of suffering than a fifty years' war. I doubt whether Great Britain could avoid convulsions.

PRINCIPLE #7
ENGINEER ELECTIONS

A s I have said, concentration of wealth yields concentration of political power, especially as the cost of elections continues to skyrocket. There is the shredding of the democratic system by the rapid increase in the ability to just buy elections. Take *Citizens United*, a very important Supreme Court decision in 2009. Now this has a history, and you've got to think about the history.

The Fourteenth Amendment has a provision that says no person's rights can be infringed without due process of law (actually the wording is also in the Fifth Amendment, but it was extended in the Fourteenth Amendment), and the intent, clearly, was to protect freed slaves. It says, "Okay, they've got the protection of the law." I don't think it's ever been used for freed slaves—if ever, marginally. Almost immediately, it was used for businesses—corporations—their rights can't be infringed without due process of law. This is a sharp attack on classical liberal principles, and was con-

See *Citizens United v. Federal Election Commission*, Supreme Court of the United States, January 21, 2010, on page 103

demned by conservatives in those days. But that trend continued into the early twentieth century, when it was pretty much established that corporations have personal rights, and it extended through the twentieth century, when they gradually became persons under the law.

CORPORATE PERSONHOOD

Corporations are state-created legal fictions. Maybe they're good, maybe they're bad—but to call them persons is kind of outrageous. For example, take the so-called free trade agreements, say, NAFTA. They gave corporations rights *way* beyond what persons have. So if General Motors invests in Mexico, they get national rights, the rights of a Mexican business—but if a Mexican person comes to New York and says, "I want national rights," well, there's no need to say what happens. So while the notion of personhood was expanded to include corporations, it was restricted for others.

If you take the Fourteenth Amendment literally, then no undocumented alien can be deprived of rights if they're a person. Well, the courts, in their wisdom over the years, have carved that away and said they're not persons. Undocumented aliens who are living here and building your buildings, cleaning your lawns, and so on, they're not persons, but General Electric is a person, an immortal, superpowerful person. This perversion of the elementary morality, and the obvious meaning of the law, is quite incredible.

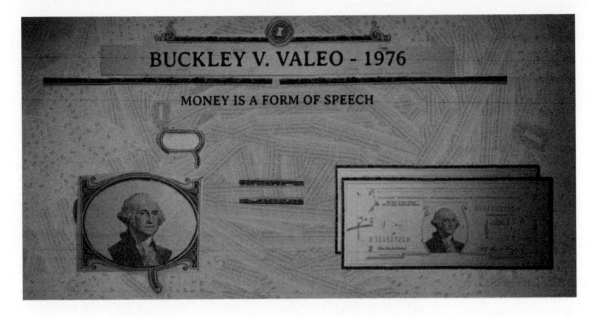

BUCKLEY V. VALEO - 1976

MONEY IS A FORM OF SPEECH

THE CORPORATE-SPONSORED ELECTION

In the 1970s, the courts decided that money was a form of speech in the ruling of *Buckley v. Valeo*. But then you go on through the years to *Citizens United*, which says the right of free speech of corporations—mainly to spend as much money as they want—that can't be curtailed. Take a look at what that means. It means that corporations, which have been pretty much buying elections anyway, are now free to do it with virtually no constraint. That's a tremendous attack on the residue of democracy.

It's very interesting to read the rulings, like Justice Kennedy's swing vote. His ruling said, "Well, look, after all, CBS is given freedom of speech—they're a corporation—why shouldn't General Electric be free to spend as much money as they want?" It's true that CBS is given freedom of speech, but they're supposed to be perform-

See *Buckley v. Valeo*, Supreme Court of the United States, January 30, 1976, on page 104

ing a *public service*. That's why. That's what the press is supposed to be, and General Electric is trying to make money for the chief executive, some of the shareholders, the other banks, and so on. And it was passed with no disclosure required—so that gives immense freedom.

It's an incredible decision, and it puts the country in a position where business power is greatly extended beyond what it always was. This is part of that vicious cycle. The Supreme Court justices are put in by reactionary presidents, who get in there because they're funded by business. It's the way the cycle works.

Thomas Ferguson, the political scientist who's the leading specialist on campaign funding, has developed what he calls "the investment theory of politics," implying that business and investors, not the voters, have tremendous influence in the political system. I mean, candidates are going

See "Revealed: Why the Pundits Are Wrong About Big Money and the 2012 Elections," AlterNet, Thomas Ferguson, Paul Jorgensen, and Jie Chen, December 20, 2012, on page 105

to continue to need billions of dollars in campaign funding and where do you go—especially after *Citizens United*, which frees up corporate funding? If you want to be in the game, you go to the center of the corporate system.

The funding for campaigns is not just to get the candidate in. If you're funding a candidate, it buys access. Every funder understands that. That candidate is going to give you privileged access, because he or she wants the funding to continue. And when the candidate wins, privileged access means that your corporate lawyers go to the staff of the legislator, the people who actually write the legislation. The legislators often don't even know what's in it, but the people who actually do the work—your corporate lawyers—go and deluge them with alleged data, arguments, and tons of material; they basically write the laws. So, what comes out as policy is pretty much what's written by corporate lobbyists and lawyers, who gain the access thanks to funding.

BEYOND THE BALLOT BOX

In my own view, the electoral extravaganza that takes place every four years should take about ten minutes of our time, literally. One minute should be spent on learning something about arithmetic. There's a very simple point about arithmetic—if you happen to be in a swing state, a state where the outcome is indefinite, and you don't vote for, say, Clinton, that's equivalent to voting for Trump. That's arithmetic. So we take one minute to settle the question of arithmetic, then we take about two minutes to look at the merits of the two parties. Not just the candidates, but the parties. My own view is that under current circumstances it should take about two minutes. And then we take the rest of the ten minutes to go to the ballot box and push a lever.

Meanwhile, after we've spent those ten minutes, we've turned to what really matters, which is not the election, but the continued effort to develop and organize active dedicated popular movements that will continue to struggle constantly for what has to be done. That's not only demonstrating, pressuring candidates, and so on—but it's also building an electoral system that means something. You don't build a better-functioning democracy, or a party for that matter, by voting once every four years.

If you want a third party, an independent party, it's not enough to vote for it every four years. You have to be out there *constantly*—developing the system that goes from school boards to city councils, legislatures, all the way up to Congress. And there are people who understand that, namely the Far Right. That's how the Tea Party got organized—with plenty of capital and plenty of thinking—and it has an effect. Those who are interested in an independent progressive party just haven't done that. They've been trapped by the propaganda that says the only thing that matters is the electoral extravaganza. You can't ignore it—it's there—but, like I say, it should take about ten minutes. But the other things—the things that really matter—they need to be done constantly.

CITIZENS UNITED V. FEDERAL ELECTION COMMISSION, 2010, AND OTHER SOURCES

Citizens United v. Federal Election Commission, Supreme Court of the United States, January 21, 2010

The law's exception for media corporations is, on its own terms, all but an admission of the invalidity of the antidistortion rationale. And the exemption results in a further, separate reason for finding this law invalid: Again by its own terms, the law exempts some corporations but covers others, even though both have the need or the motive to communicate their views. The exemption applies to media corporations owned or controlled by corporations that have diverse and substantial investments and participate in endeavors other than news. So even assuming the most doubtful proposition that a news organization has a right to speak when others do not, the exemption would allow a conglomerate that owns both a media business and an unrelated business to influence or control the media in order to advance its overall business interest. At the same time, some other corporation, with an identical business interest but no media outlet in its ownership structure, would be forbidden to speak or inform the public about the same issue. This differential treatment cannot be squared with the First Amendment.

Buckley v. Valeo, Supreme Court of the United States, January 30, 1976

A restriction on the amount of money a person or group can spend on political communication during a campaign necessarily reduces the quantity of expression by restricting the number of issues discussed, the depth of their exploration, and the size of the audience reached. This is because virtually every means of communicating ideas in today's mass society requires the expenditure of money. The distribution of the humblest handbill or leaflet entails printing, paper, and circulation costs. Speeches and rallies generally necessitate hiring a hall and publicizing the event. The electorate's increasing dependence on television, radio, and other mass media for news and information has made these expensive modes of communication indispensable instruments of effective political speech.

"Revealed: Why the Pundits Are Wrong About Big Money and the 2012 Elections," AlterNet, Thomas Ferguson, Paul Jorgensen, and Jie Chen, December 20, 2012

For now we remind readers that the dynamics of campaigns funded mostly by major investors are quite different than the campaigns imagined by traditional democratic theory: "Big Money's most significant impact on politics is certainly not to deliver elections to the highest bidders. Instead it is to cement parties, candidates, and campaigns into the narrow range of issues that are acceptable to big donors. The basis of the 'Golden Rule' in politics derives from the simple fact that running for major office in the U.S. is fabulously expensive. In the absence of large scale social movements, only political positions that can be financed can be presented to voters. On issues on which all major investors agree (think of the now famous 1 percent), no party competition at all takes place, even if everyone knows that heavy majorities of voters want something else."

LIBERTY

PANEL

3

5700
PIECES

fig. 1

FIG. 23

FIG. 24

FIG. 27

FIG. 26

FIG. 25

FIG. 28   FIG. 29   FIG. 30   FIG. 31

FIG. 32

KEEP THE RABBLE
IN LINE

THERE IS one organized force that, with all its flaws, has traditionally been in the forefront of efforts to improve the lives of the general population. That's organized labor. It's the one barrier to this vicious cycle going on, which leads to corporate tyranny.

A major reason for the concentrated, almost fanatic attack on unions and organized labor is they are a democratizing force. They provide a barrier that defends workers' rights, but also popular rights generally. That interferes with the prerogatives and power of those who own and manage the society.

I should say that antiunion sentiment in the United States among elites is so strong that the fundamental core of labor rights—the basic principle in the International

Labor Organization, which is the right of free association, hence the right to form unions—has never been ratified by the US. I think the US may be alone among major societies in that respect. It's considered so far out of the spectrum of American politics that it literally has never been considered.

The business class is highly class-conscious, and rising popular power has always called forth real, deep concerns on the part of the business classes and the educated sectors, which are usually in line with the thesis that "too much democracy" is a real problem. Remember, the US has a long and very violent labor history as compared with similar societies. The labor movement had been very strong, but by the 1920s, in a period not unlike today, it was virtually crushed—in part by Woodrow Wilson's red scare, in part by other means. (One of the great labor historians, David Montgomery, describes this in one of his main books, *The Fall of the House of Labor*).

See "Ford Men Beat and Rout Lewis Union Organizers; 80,000 Out in Steel Strike; 16 Hurt in Battle," *New York Times*, May 26, 1937, on page 117

So, the labor movement was really pretty dormant right through the early '30s, but by the mid-'30s, it began to reconstruct. The organization of the CIO (Congress of Industrial Organizations) was the most significant part, and it drew in lots of people. It had a galvanizing effect on other kinds of activism, along with, we're not supposed to say it today, but along with the Communist Party, which was the spearhead of all kinds of activism—civil rights, labor organizing, social and political movements, and so on.

THE NEW DEAL

Franklin Delano Roosevelt was rather sympathetic to progressive legislation that would benefit the general population, but he had to somehow get it passed. He informed labor leaders and others, "Force me to do it. If you can force me to do it, I'll be glad to do it." What he meant is, go out and demonstrate, organize, protest, develop the labor movement, strike, and so on. When the popular pressure is sufficient, I'll be able to put through the legislation you want. So there was kind of a combination of a sympathetic government that was interested in overcoming the tremendous shock and disaster of the Depression—again, caused by a financial crisis that they were interested in overcoming—and developing legislation that would benefit the general public.

The business world was actually split during the New Deal years, the 1930s. High-tech internationally oriented business was supportive of the New Deal. They didn't object to having labor rights, decent wages, and so on. They liked the international orientation of the New Deal government. The National Association of Manufacturers, which is a much more labor-intensive industry, much more domestically oriented, they were passionately opposed to the New Deal. So there was a split among the masters. For example, the head of General Electric was one of the major supporters of Roosevelt. And that helped, along with the massive popular uprising, to enable Roosevelt to carry through the highly successful

See "Harry Truman, address in Louisville, Kentucky," September 30, 1948, on page 118

New Deal legislations. This laid the basis for postwar economic growth, as well as overcoming some of the worst effects of the Depression. Not joblessness, however—that remained until the Second World War.

So there was kind of a combination of sympathetic government and, by the mid-'30s, very substantial popular activism. There were industrial actions. There were sit-down strikes, which were very frightening to ownership. You have to recognize the sit-down strike is just one step before saying, "We don't need bosses. We can run this by ourselves." And business was appalled. You read the business press in the late '30s, and they were talking about "the hazard facing industrialists in the rising political power of the masses," which has to be repressed. We must fight the "everlasting battle for the minds of men to indoctrinate people with the capitalist story," and on and on. It sounds kind of vulgar Marxist, but the business classes tend to be vulgar Marxist, fighting the class war. The business literature in the 1930s, actually, kind of reads like the *Powell Memorandum*: "we're lost, everything's being destroyed." In fact, the business world began to develop what were called at that time scientific methods of strike breaking. Violence isn't working anymore, we can't do it, so let's look at more sophisticated ways to undermine the labor movement.

The Depression itself wasn't really ended until the Second World War, when there was a huge government stimulus that led to a vast increase in industrial production—it practically quadrupled—and sent people back to work. It set the stage for the unprecedented postwar growth and development, with quite substantial government inputs. (Computers, the Internet, things that a lot of people take for granted now—you look back and they developed substantially through what amounts to the state sector of the economy. Most of the high-tech economy developed that way.)

THE BUSINESS OFFENSIVE

So, things were on hold during the Second World War, but immediately afterward, the business offensive began in force. The Taft-Hartley Act and McCarthyism, for instance, were followed by massive corporate propaganda offensives—offensives to attack unions, to take over and control the educational system, sports leagues, infiltrate churches, everything—it was just massive. There's a lot of good scholarship on this.

Going along with this was getting people to have a more ambivalent attitude toward government. On the one hand, people must be induced to hate and fear government, the potential instrument of popular will, while private corporations are left unaccountable, yielding a form of tyranny—the more they have power and the less government has power, the better from the viewpoint of the rich and powerful. So on the one hand, people have to be induced to hate government, while on the other hand, they have to support government because private business relies extensively on state support—all the way

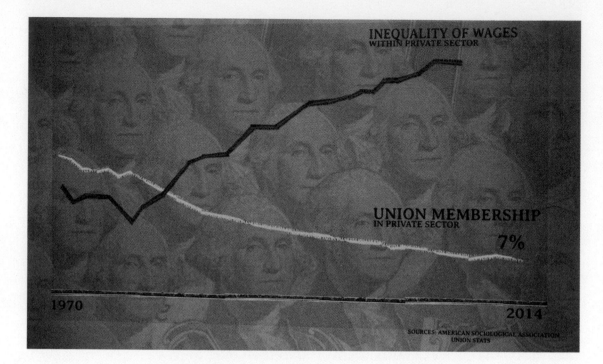

INEQUALITY OF WAGES
WITHIN PRIVATE SECTOR

UNION MEMBERSHIP
IN PRIVATE SECTOR

7%

1970

2014

SOURCES: AMERICAN SOCIOLOGICAL ASSOCIATION
UNION STATS

from high-technology economy to bailouts, to international force, and so on—a vast spectrum.

The offensive increased sharply during the Reagan years. Reagan pretty much told the business world, "If you want to illegally break organizing efforts and strikes, go ahead"— and, in fact, illegal strike breaking shot way up, and illegal firing tripled. Even before, in 1978, the head of the United Auto Workers, Doug Fraser, lamented the fact that, as he put it, "business is waging a one-sided class war against the working class." It continued in the '90s, and of course with George W. Bush it went through the roof. By now, less than 7 percent of private sector workers have unions, and it's not because workers don't want unions—polls show that, overwhelmingly, they want to unionize—but they can't.

See Douglas Fraser's resignation letter from the Labor-Management Group, July 17, 1978, on page 119

A few years ago we saw a dramatic illustration of public support for unions—in Madison, Wisconsin, and several other states in 2011—where efforts to really kill off the last remnants of the labor movement by Governor Walker, his super-rich backers, the Koch brothers, and the Republican legislature led to massive public protests. In Madison there were tens of thousands of people on the streets every day, "occupying" the State Capitol. They had enormous popular support. Polls showed a considerable majority of the population supported them. It wasn't enough to beat back the legislative efforts, but if that continues it could very well lead to the kind of situation in which a sympathetic government could respond by implementing policies that would deal with the real problems of the country (and not the ones that are of concern to the financial institutions). The effect of the business postwar offensive is that the usual counterforce to an assault by our highly class-conscious business class has dissolved.

THE NEW SPIRIT OF THE AGE

If you're in a position of power, you want to maintain class consciousness for yourself, but eliminate it everywhere else. You go back to the nineteenth century, in the early days of the Industrial Revolution in the United States, working people were very conscious of this. They overwhelmingly regarded wage labor as not very different from slavery, different only in that it was *temporary*. In fact, it was such a popular idea that it was a slogan of the Republican Party. That's the idea under which Northern workers went to war in the Civil War—they wanted to eliminate all kinds of chattel slavery in the South, wage slavery in the North. "Working people ought to take over the factories" was the slogan of the big mass labor organizations that were developing.

This goes way back in American history, and the sources are interesting. One hundred and fifty years ago, in the early days of the Industrial Revolution, there was a very free press. For example, working people ran their own newspapers, in factories and elsewhere, mainly around eastern New England. Now there are some constant themes that ran through that press. There was a bitter attack on the industrial system, which they said was turning free Americans into basically slaves. Wage labor was regarded as not very different from slavery, but the striking theme was anger at what some called, and I'm quoting now, "the New Spirit of the Age, gain wealth forgetting all but self." And this is the mid-nineteenth century. That's the "New Spirit" 150 years ago—you get wealthy, forget about everyone else. That was a very sharp class consciousness. In the interest of power and privilege, it's good to drive those ideas out of people's heads. You don't want them to know that they're an oppressed class. You get the situation we are in now where "class" has become a dirty word—you can't say it.

See "Factory Tracts," the "Mill Girls" of Lowell, Massachusetts, 1845, on page 121

You've all studied the first paragraph of Adam Smith's *Wealth of Nations*, about the butcher, the baker, everybody works together and division of labor is wonderful. But not many people have gotten to, say, page 450 where he sharply condemns division of labor, because he says it turns people into creatures as stupid and ignorant as can be, because they're gonna be driven to performing routine, simple tasks, and not developing and exercising their intelligence and creative capacity. So, therefore, he urges that in every civilized society the government intervene to prevent this from happening.

We're human beings, we're not automatons. You work at your job but you don't stop being a human being. Being a human being means benefiting from rich cultural traditions—not just our own traditions, but many others—and becoming not just skilled, but also wise. Somebody who can think—think creatively, think independently, explore, inquire—and contribute to society. If you don't have that, you might as well be replaced by a robot. I think that simply can't be ignored if we want to have a society that's worth living in.

Another unpronounceable word incidentally is "profits," so when you hear a politician say, "we've got to have jobs," think about it for a minute. It almost always translates into "we have to have profits." They don't care about jobs—the same people who are saying "we have to have jobs" are happily exporting them to Mexico and China, because that increases profits—what they're really after. The whole rhetorical system has shifted around to try to prevent people from seeing what's happening—that's understandable, and exactly what you'd expect people with power to do, but we should recognize it.

CLASS CONSCIOUSNESS

Actually, the US has less social mobility than comparable industrial countries, but if you start talking about class, people begin to think about that. In fact, I have a friend who teaches introductory history courses in a state college, and she asks her students when they come in to identify their class background, and gets two standard answers: if your father is in jail you're underclass, if your father is a janitor you're middle class. Now those are the only categories, either you're underclass or middle class. When we're talking about working people, we mostly refer to them as middle class. And as I have said before, the middle class, in that sense—that unique American sense—is under severe attack.

So this is one of the few societies in which you just don't talk about class. Last time I looked, the census did not even rank people by class. In fact, the notion of class is pretty simple: Who gives the orders? Who follows them? That basically defines class. It's more nuanced and complex, but that's basically it.

We're not genetically different from the people in the 1930s. What was done then can be done again. And remember that, at that time, it was done after a period not unlike today—a period of very high inequality, harsh repression, destruction of the labor movement, a much poorer society than today with fewer opportunities. We can pick up the same thing, and turn the current developments in that direction. But it's gotta be done. It's not gonna happen by itself.

"FORD MEN BEAT AND ROUT . . . ," 1937, AND OTHER SOURCES

"Ford Men Beat and Rout Lewis Union Organizers; 80,000 Out in Steel Strike; 16 Hurt in Battle," *New York Times*, May 26, 1937

An outburst of violence, in which union representatives were beaten, kicked and driven away, marked today the first attempt of the United Automobile Workers of America to organize the employees of the Ford Motor Company.

Richard T. Frankensteen, directing the membership drive on behalf of the auto affiliate of the Committee for Industrial

Organization, and Walter Reuther, president of the West Side local of the automobile workers' union, were set upon by a group of employees at No.4 gate of the Ford Rouge plant in Dearborn. With two other men who had accompanied them to oversee the distribution of union handbills, they were knocked down repeatedly, kicked, and finally forced away from the gate, despite efforts of Frankensteen to fight off his assailants.

Subsequent fighting, in which employees routed union representatives who had come to distribute leaflets, resulted in the injury of twelve more persons, seven of them women, the union stated.

"It was the worst licking I've ever taken," Frankensteen declared. "They bounced us down the concrete steps of an overpass we had climbed. Then they would knock us down, stand us up, and knock us down again."

Both Frankensteen and Reuther, together with several of the other victims, were treated by physicians.

Harry Truman, address in Louisville, Kentucky, September 30, 1948

We know how the NAM [National Association of Manufacturers] organized this conspiracy against the American consumer. One of its own officers was so proud of the work they did that he spilled the story in an interview, which was published after price control was killed. Now listen to this very carefully.

In this interview, the Director of Public Relations of the NAM told how his organization spent $3,000,000 in 1946 to destroy OPA [Office of Price Administration]. The NAM spent a million and a half on newspaper advertising. They sent their own speakers to make a thousand talks before women's clubs, civic organizations, teachers, another one to 15,000 clergymen, another one to 35,000 farm leaders, and still another to 40,000 leaders of women's clubs. A special clip sheet with NAM propaganda went to 7,500 weekly newspapers and to 2,500 columnists and editorial writers.

There never was a more vicious or a better organized campaign to mislead and deceive the American people.

Douglas Fraser's resignation letter from the Labor-Management Group, July 17, 1978

Dear Labor-Management Group Member:

. . . I have come to the reluctant conclusion that my participation in the Labor-Management Group cannot continue. I am therefore resigning from the Group as of July 19 . . .

I have concluded that participation in these meetings is no longer useful to me or to the 1.5 million workers I represent as president of the UAW. I believe leaders of the business community, with few exceptions, have chosen to wage a one-sided class war today in this country—a war against working people, the unemployed, the poor, the minorities, the very young and the very old, and even many in the middle class of our society. The leaders of industry, commerce and finance in the United States have broken and discarded the fragile, unwritten compact previously existing during a past period of growth and progress.

For a considerable time, the leaders of business and labor have sat at the Labor-Management Group's table—recognizing differences, but seeking consensus where it existed. That worked because the business community in the U.S. succeeded in advocating a general loyalty to an allegedly benign capitalism that emphasized private property, independence and self-regulation along with an allegiance to free, democratic politics.

That system has worked best, of course, for the "haves" in our society rather than the "have-nots." Yet it survived in part because of an unspoken foundation: that when things got bad enough for a segment of society, the business elite "gave" a little bit—enabling government or interest groups to better conditions somewhat for that segment. That give usually came only after sustained struggle, such as that waged by the labor movement in the 1930s and the civil rights movement in the 1960s . . .

The latest breakdown in our relationship is also perhaps the most serious. The fight waged by the business community against that Labor Law Reform bill stands as the most vicious, unfair attack upon the labor movement in more than 30 years . . . Labor law reform itself would not have organized a single worker. Rather, it would have begun to limit the ability of certain rogue employers to keep workers from choosing democratically to be represented by unions through employer delay and outright violation of existing labor law . . .

The rise of multinational corporations that know neither patriotism nor morality but only self-interest, has made accountability almost non-existent. At virtually every level, I discern a demand by business for docile government and unrestrained corporate individualism. Where industry once yearned for subservient unions, it now wants no unions at all.

"Factory Tracts," the "Mill Girls" of Lowell, Massachusetts, 1845

When you sell your product, you retain your person. But when you sell your labour, you sell yourself, losing the rights of free men and becoming vassals of mammoth establishments of a monied aristocracy that threatens annihilation to anyone who questions their right to enslave and oppress. Those who work in the mills ought to own them, not have the status of machines ruled by private despots who are entrenching monarchic principles on democratic soil as they drive downwards freedom and rights, civilization, health, morals and intellectuality in the new commercial feudalism.

PRINCIPLE #9
MANUFACTURE CONSENT

O NE OF the first major modern studies of the nature
of government was by David Hume, a great philosopher and political philosopher as well. He wrote on
what he called the "foundations of the theory of government," and one thing he pointed out was that in every
state, no matter what type—whether it's feudal, milita-
ristic, whatever it was—"power is in the hands of the
governed." They can, if they get together, take power.
As long as they can be made to feel that they don't have
power, then the powerful can rule. But if they come to
understand that they *do* have power, then repressive and
authoritarian governments alike will collapse. That's one
of the reasons why we have this enormous public relations industry.

See *Essays, Moral, Political, Literary,* David Hume, 1741, on page 131

THE RISE OF THE PR INDUSTRY

The public relations industry is a phenomenon that developed in the freest countries, in Britain and the United States, and the reason is pretty clear. A century ago it became clear that it was not going to be so easy to control the population by force. Too much freedom had been won through labor organizing, parliamentary Labor parties in many countries, women starting to get the franchise, and so on. It was kind of like the '60s, the danger of democracy, and the reaction was sort of similar. A crucial part of it was the rise of the PR industry.

Its leading intellectual figure and kind of guru was Edward Bernays, a Wilson/Roosevelt/Kennedy progressive talking from the so-called left end of the political spectrum. He wrote a book called *Propaganda*—the term was used honestly in those days—which was a kind of manual, providing theoretical guidance for the rising public relations industry. He explained the purpose in kind of Madisonian terms. He said the country has to be governed by the "intelligent minority," which is of course *us*—anyone who advocates this is part of it. So the intelligent minority has to run the country in the interests of the general population. You can't let them make the decisions, because they'll make terrible decisions. Part of the way we do this is by what he called "engineering of consent." They're too dumb to understand so we'll engineer their consent to what we decide, and that's the purpose of the public relations industry.

See *Propaganda*, Edward Bernays, 1928, on page 132

You find this doctrine all through progressive intellectual thought, like Walter Lippmann, the major progressive intellectual of the twentieth century. He wrote famous progressive essays on democracy in which his view was exactly that. "The public must be put in their place" so that the responsible men can make decisions without interference from the "bewildered herd."

FABRICATING CONSUMERS

It was understood and expressed that you have to control people through beliefs and attitudes. Well, one of the best ways to control people in terms of attitudes is by what the great political economist Thorstein Veblen called "fabricating consumers." If you can fabricate wants, make obtaining things that are just about within your reach the essence of life, they're going to be trapped into becoming consumers. You read the business press in the 1920s and it talks about the need to direct people to the superficial things of life, like "fashionable consumption," and that'll keep them out of our hair.

In fact, Bernays had major achievements in his lifetime that are worth looking at. The first of them was to get women to smoke. Women didn't smoke in those days, and he organized big publicity campaigns—I think in those days it was for Chesterfield, around 1930—to convince women that smoking was what we would today call "cool." You know, proper, something a model liberated woman would do, and so on. No one can calculate how

See "From Social Taboo to 'Torch of Freedom': The Marketing of Cigarettes to Women," Amanda Amos and Margaretha Haglund, 2000, on page 133

many tens of millions of deaths you can attribute to that success. (Another major success of his was in the 1950s, when he was working for the United Fruit Company, and convinced people to overthrow the democratic government of Guatemala—because it was threatening company control over the economy and the society—which led to over fifty years of horrors and atrocities).

Now these are elite concepts that run right through history. The advertising industry just exploded with this goal—fabricating consumers, trapping people into consumerism—and it's done with great sophistication. The ideal is what you actually see today where, let's say, teenage girls if they have a free Saturday afternoon will go walking in the shopping mall, not to the library or somewhere else. Kids will feel, "I haven't achieved anything in my life unless I have another electronic gadget."

The idea is to try to control *everyone*, to turn the whole society into the perfect system. The perfect system would be a society based on a *dyad*—a pair. The pair is you and your television set, or maybe now you and your iPhone and the Internet, and that presents you with what the proper life would be—what kinds of gadgets you should have, what you should do for your health. Then you spend your time and effort gaining those things that you don't need or don't want—maybe you'll throw them away—but that's the measure of a decent life.

IRRATIONAL CHOICES

If you've ever taken an economics course you know that markets are supposed to be based on informed consumers making rational choices. I don't have to tell you, that's not what's done. If advertisers lived by market principles then some enterprise, say, General Motors, would put on a brief announcement of their products and their properties, along with comments by *Consumer Reports* magazine so you could make a judgment about it.

That's not what an ad for a car is—an ad for a car is a football hero, an actress, the car doing some crazy thing like going up a mountain or something. If you've ever turned on your television set, you know that hundreds of millions of dollars are spent to try to create *uninformed* consumers who will make *irrational* choices—that's what advertising is.

Some years ago it came to be recognized in the advertising industry that there's a sector of the population that they're not reaching—children. Children don't have any money so they hadn't been directing advertising to children. It was understood that that's a mistake. Children may not have money but their parents do. So something new developed in the advertising industry—it's called "the psychology of nagging." So, applied psychology departments now, in the academic world, study various kinds of nagging—if the advertiser wants the kids to nag for this thing, they'll advertise in a particular way; if you want them to nag for a different thing, they'll advertise another way.

See *Fast Food Nation: The Dark Side of the All-American Meal*, Eric Schlosser, 2001, on page 134

Parents are familiar with this because they see it happening. When I watch television with my grandchildren, by the time they're two years old they're being inundated with propaganda—what their parents have to buy them. It starts from childhood, and you can see it clearly. Actually, there are good studies of the effects of this on children and adults as they grow up. So that's one form of trapping people.

Another very significant form of trapping people is by debt. It wasn't invented here, and it has an interesting history. You go back to the 1830s, when the British were abandoning slavery in their colonies and they had a problem. What are you going to do when the slaves are free? How are you going to keep them working on the plantations? After all, there's plenty of land and they can go off, get themselves a patch of land, and live quite happily. Well, they hit on the same method. What we have to do is trap them into consumerism. Carry out enough propaganda and teasers and so on to make freed slaves feel they've got to have these commodities. They go to the company store and they get them, they're in debt, and pretty soon they're trapped—the slave economy's back.

See *Twice the Work of Free Labor: The Political Economy of Convict Labor in the New South,* Alex Lichtenstein, 1996, on page 136

UNDERMINING ELECTIONS

When the same institutions—the PR system—run elections, they do it the same way. They want to create an uninformed electorate that will make irrational choices, often against their own interests.

Democracy is supposed to be based on informed citizens making rational decisions. But the PR industry runs the campaigns so that all you get is glitz, and illusion, and personalities, and so on. Keep away from issues—and the reason that you have to keep away from issues is clear enough. On issues there's a big, substantial divide between public policy and public opinion. So let's drive the population to marginal things, and that way we can undermine democracy the same way we undermine markets—and also contribute to the general purpose of marginalizing, atomizing people and directing their attitudes and concerns away from what might matter to them as functioning people in a free, vibrant, democratic society to just working for us.

They're to be spectators, not participants. Then you get a "properly functioning democracy"—straight back to Madison and on to the *Powell Memorandum* and so on. And we see it every time one of these extravaganzas takes place.

SELLING CANDIDATES

Right after the election, President Obama won an award from the advertising industry for the best marketing campaign of 2008. It wasn't reported here, but if you go to the international business press, executives were euphoric. They said, "We've been selling candidates, marketing candidates like toothpaste ever since Reagan, and this is the greatest achievement we have."

See "Obama Wins! . . . Ad Age's Marketer of the Year," *Advertising Age,* Matthew Creamer, October 17, 2008, on page 136

I don't usually agree with Sarah Palin, but when she mocks what she calls the "hopey changey stuff"—she's right. First of all, Obama didn't really promise anything, that's mostly illusion. Go back to the campaign rhetoric and take a look at it. There's very little discussion of policy issues, and for very good reason—because public opinion on policy is sharply disconnected from what the leadership of the two parties and their financial backers want. Policy, more and more, is focused on the private interests that fund the campaigns—with the public being marginalized.

If you think about it, the advertising industry—which spends hundreds of millions of dollars a year to create the kind of individual who's focused on fulfilling artificial, externally imposed wants, and who is an uninformed consumer making irrational decisions—the reason they're spending huge funds on that is because they believe people are rational. Otherwise, they wouldn't bother. They're trying to turn people into irrational creatures, and they're putting huge efforts into it. And I think they're right. They're not wasting their money. If they didn't do that, people would be making rational decisions, and I think the rational decisions would be, essentially, dismantling illegitimate authority and hierarchic institutions.

ESSAYS, MORAL, POLITICAL, LITERARY, 1741, AND OTHER SOURCES

Essays, Moral, Political, Literary, David Hume, 1741

Nothing appears more surprizing to those, who consider human affairs with a philosophical eye, than the easiness with which the many are governed by the few; and the implicit submission, with which men resign their own sentiments and passions to those of their rulers. When we enquire by what means this wonder is effected, we shall find, that, as FORCE is always on the side of the governed, the governors have nothing to support them but opinion. It is therefore, on opinion only that government is founded; and this maxim extends to the most despotic and most military governments, as well as to the most free and most popular. The soldan of EGYPT, or the emperor of ROME, might drive his harmless subjects, like brute beasts, against their sentiments and inclination: But he must, at least, have led his *mamalukes*, or *praetorian bands*, like men, by their opinion.

Propaganda, Edward Bernays, 1928

The conscious and intelligent manipulation of the organized habits and opinions of the masses is an important element in democratic society. Those who manipulate this unseen mechanism of society constitute an invisible government which is the true ruling power of our country.

We are governed, our minds are molded, our tastes formed, our ideas suggested, largely by men we have never heard of. This is a logical result of the way in which our democratic society is organized. Vast numbers of human beings must cooperate in this manner if they are to live together as a smoothly functioning society . . .

They govern us by their qualities of natural leadership, their ability to supply needed ideas and by their key position in the social structure. Whatever attitude one chooses to take toward this condition, it remains a fact that in almost every act of our daily lives, whether in the sphere of politics or business, in our social conduct or our ethical thinking, we are dominated by the relatively small number of persons—a trifling fraction of our hundred and twenty million—who understand the mental processes and social patterns of the masses. It is they who pull the wires which control the public mind, who harness old social forces and contrive new ways to bind and guide the world . . .

Ours must be a leadership democracy administered by the intelligent minority who know how to regiment and guide the masses.

Is this government by propaganda? Call it, if you prefer, government by education. But education, in the academic sense of the word, is not sufficient. It must be enlightened expert propaganda through the creation of circumstances, through the high-spotting of significant events, and the dramatization of important issues. The statesman of the future will thus be enabled to focus the public mind on crucial points of policy, and regiment a vast, heterogeneous mass of voters to clear understanding and intelligent action.

"From Social Taboo to 'Torch of Freedom': The Marketing of Cigarettes to Women," Amanda Amos and Margaretha Haglund, 2000

[I]t is questionable whether smoking would have become as popular among women as it did if tobacco companies had not seized on this opportunity in the 1920s and

1930s to exploit ideas of liberation, power, and other important values for women to recruit them to the cigarette market. In particular they needed to develop new social images and meanings for female smoking to overcome the association with louche and libidinous behaviour and morals. Smoking had to be repositioned as not only respectable but sociable, fashionable, stylish, and feminine. The goal was a potential doubling of the market. As described in 1928 by Mr Hill, the president of American Tobacco, "It will be like opening a new gold mine right in our front yard".

Fast Food Nation:
The Dark Side of the All-American Meal,
Eric Schlosser, 2001

The explosion in children's advertising occurred during the 1980s. Many working parents, feeling guilty about spending less time with their kids, started spending more money on them. One marketing expert has called the 1980s "the decade of the child consumer." After largely ignoring children for years, Madison Avenue began to scrutinize and pursue them. Major ad agencies now have children's divisions, and a variety of marketing firms focus solely on kids. These groups tend to have sweet-sounding names: Small Talk, Kid Connection, Kid2Kid, the Geppetto Group, Just Kids, Inc. At least three industry publications—*Youth*

Market Alert, *Selling to Kids*, and *Marketing to Kids Report*—cover the latest ad campaigns and market research. The growth in children's advertising has been driven by efforts to increase not just current, but also future, consumption. Hoping that nostalgic childhood memories of a brand will lead to a lifetime of purchases, companies now plan "cradle-to-grave" advertising strategies. They have come to believe what Ray Kroc and Walt Disney realized long ago—a person's "brand loyalty" may begin as early as the age of two. Indeed, market research has found that children often recognize a brand logo before they can recognize their own name . . .

The bulk of the advertising directed at children today has an immediate goal. "It's not just getting kids to whine," one marketer explained in *Selling to Kids*, "it's giving them a specific reason to ask for the product." Years ago sociologist Vance Packard described children as "surrogate salesmen" who had to persuade other people, usually their parents, to buy what they wanted. Marketers now use different terms to explain the intended response to their ads—such as "leverage," "the nudge factor," "pester power." The aim of most children's advertising is straightforward: Get kids to nag their parents and nag them well.

Twice the Work of Free Labor: The Political Economy of Convict Labor in the New South, Alex Lichtenstein, 1996

Like plantation societies throughout the nineteenth-century world, the abolition of slavery and challenge of free labor relations encouraged landed classes to seek new forms of control over agricultural labor. In all post-emancipation societies the balance between the possibility of land ownership and self-sufficiency for ex-slaves and their dependence on wager labor determined the tightness of this labor control. In the US South planters effectively transformed ex-slaves into an agricultural proletariat with a gamut of labor relations ranging from tenancy to sharecropping to debt-peonage. The necessary political corollary of this labor system was the preservation of white supremacy.

"Obama Wins! . . . Ad Age's Marketer of the Year," *Advertising Age*, Matthew Creamer, October 17, 2008

Just weeks before he demonstrates whether his campaign's blend of grass-roots appeal and big media-budget know-how has converted the American electorate, Sen. Barack Obama has shown he's already won over the nation's brand builders. He's been named *Advertising Age*'s marketer of the year for 2008.

Mr. Obama won the vote of hundreds of marketers, agency heads and marketing-services vendors gathered here at the Association of National Advertisers' annual conference . . . "I honestly look at [Obama's] campaign and I look at it as something that we can all learn from as marketers," said Angus Macaulay, VP-Rodale marketing solutions.

PRINCIPLE #10
MARGINALIZE THE POPULATION

O NE OF the leading political scientists, Martin Gilens, has done important studies of the relationship between public attitudes and public policy, based on polling data. It's a pretty straightforward thing to study—policy you can see, and public opinion you know from extensive polling. In one study, together with another fine political scientist, Benjamin Page, Gilens took about 1,700 policy decisions, and compared them with public attitudes and business interests. What they show, I think convincingly, is that policy is uncorrelated with public attitudes, and closely correlated with corporate interests. Elsewhere he showed that about 70 percent of the population has no influence on policy—they might as well be in some other country. And as you go up the income and wealth level, the impact on public policy is greater—the rich essentially get what they want.

See "Testing Theories of American Politics: Elites, Interest Groups, and Average Citizens," Martin Gilens and Benjamin I. Page, 2014, on page 151

Polling data is not refined enough for him to look beyond the top 10 percent, which is kind of misleading because the real concentration of power is in a fraction of 1 percent. But if the study was carried up to there, it's pretty clear what you'd find: they get exactly what they want, because they're basically running the place.

The fact that policy doesn't correspond to public interest shouldn't come as a big surprise. This has been going on for a long time. Government policy is designed to implement state power and the power of dominant elements within the society. Here, it means mainly the corporate sector. The welfare of the population is secondary, and often not cared for at all. And the population knows it. That's why you have this tremendous antagonism toward institutions—all institutions. So, support of Congress is often in the single digits; the presidency is disliked; corporations are disliked; banks are hated—it extends all over. Even science is disliked—"why should we believe them?"

UNFOCUSED ANGER

There's popular mobilization and activism, but in very self-destructive directions. It's taking the form of unfocused anger—hatred, attacks on one another and on vulnerable targets. Really irrational attitudes—people mobilizing against their own interests, *literally* against their own interests. Supporting political figures whose goal is to harm them as much as possible. We're seeing this right in front of us—you look at the television and the Internet, you see it every day. That's what happens in cases like this. It is corrosive of social relations, but *that's the point*. The point is to make people hate and fear each other, look out only for themselves, and not do anything for anyone else.

So take Donald Trump. For many years, I have been writing and speaking about the danger of the rise of an honest and charismatic ideologue in the United States, someone who could exploit the fear and anger that has long been boiling in much of the society, and who could direct it away from the actual agents of malaise to vulnerable targets. The dangers, however, have been real for many years, perhaps even more so in the light of the forces that Trump has unleashed, even though Trump himself does not fit the image of honest ideologue. He seems to have very little of a considered ideology apart from *me* and *my* friends.

He got huge support from people who are angry at everything. Every time Trump makes a nasty comment about whoever, his popularity goes up. Because it is based on hate and fear. The phenomenon that we are seeing here is "generalized rage." Mostly white, working-class, lower-middle-class people, who have been cast by the wayside during the neoliberalism period. They've lived through a generation of stagnation and decline. And a decline in the functioning of democracy. Even their own elected representatives barely reflect their interests and concerns. Everything has been taken away from them. There is no economic growth for them, there is for other people. The institutions are all against them. They have serious contempt for institutions, especially Congress. They have a deep concern that they are losing their country because a "generalized they" are taking it away from them. That kind of scapegoating of those who are even more vulnerable and oppressed, along with illusions about how they are being coddled by the "liberal elites," is all too familar, along with the often bitter outcomes. And it's important to bear in mind that the genuine fears and concerns can be addressed by serious and constructive policies. Many of the Trump supporters voted for Obama in 2008, believing the message of "hope and change." They saw little of either, and now in their disillusionment they are seduced by a con man offering a different message of hope and change—which could lead to a very ugly reaction when the imagery collapses. But the outcomes could be far more hopeful if there is a real and meaningful program that genuinely inspires hope and does promise seriously to bring about badly needed change. The response instead is generalized anger at everything.

One place you see it strikingly is on April 15. April 15 is kind of a measure—the day you pay your taxes—of how democratic the society is. If a society is really democratic, April 15 should be a day of celebration. It's a day when the population gets together to decide to fund the programs and activities that they have formulated and agreed upon. What could be better than that? You should celebrate it.

It's not the way it is in the United States. It's a day of mourning. It's a day in which some alien power that has nothing to do with you is coming down to steal your hard-earned money—and you do everything you can to keep them from doing it. That's a measure of the extent to which, at least in popular consciousness, democracy is actually functioning. Not a very attractive picture.

The tendencies that we've been describing within American society, unless reversed, will create an extremely ugly society. A society that's based on Adam Smith's vile maxim, "All for ourselves, nothing for anyone else," the New Spirit of the Age, "gain wealth, forgetting all but self," a society in which normal human instincts and emotions of sympathy, solidarity, mutual support, in which they're driven out. That's a society so ugly I don't even know who'd want to live in it. I wouldn't want my children to.

If a society is based on control by private wealth, it will reflect those values—values of greed and the desire to maximize personal gain at the expense of others. Now, a small society based on that principle is ugly, but it can survive. A global society based on that principle is headed for massive destruction.

THE SURVIVAL OF THE SPECIES

I think the future looks pretty grim. I mean, we are facing really serious problems. There's one thing that shouldn't be ignored—we're in a stage of history for the first time ever where we're facing literal questions of species survival. Can the species survive, at least in any decent form? That's a real problem.

On November 8, 2016, the most powerful country in world history, which will set its stamp on what comes next, had an election. The outcome placed total control of the government—executive, Congress, the Supreme Court—in the hands of the Republican Party, which has become the most dangerous organization in world history.

Apart from the last phrase, all of this is uncontroversial. The last phrase may seem outlandish, even outrageous. But is it? The facts suggest otherwise. The party is dedicated to racing as rapidly as possible to destruction of organized human life. There is no historical precedent for such a stand.

Is this an exaggeration? Consider what we have just been witnessing. The winning candidate calls for rapid increase in use of fossil fuels, including coal; dismantling of regulations; rejection of help to developing countries that are seeking to move to sustainable energy; and in general, racing to the cliff as fast as possible.

And there have already been direct consequences. The COP21 Paris negotiations on climate change aimed for a verifiable treaty, but had to settle for verbal commitments because the Republican Congress would not accept any binding commitments. The follow-up COP22 Marrakech conference aimed to fill in the gaps. It opened on November 7, 2016. On November 8, election day, the World Meteorological Organization presented a dire and ominous report on the current state of environmental destruction. As the results of the election came in, the conference turned to the question of whether the whole process could continue with the most powerful country withdrawing from it and seeking to undermine it. The conference ended with no issue—and an astonishing spectacle. The leader in upholding the hopes for decent survival was China! And the leading wrecker, in virtual isolation, was "the leader of the Free World." One can, again, hardly find words to capture this spectacle.

It is no less difficult to find words to capture the utterly astonishing fact that in all the massive coverage of the electoral extravaganza, none of this receives more than passing mention. At least I am at a loss to find appropriate words.

We are heading, eyes open, toward a world in which our grandchildren may not even be able to survive. We're heading toward environmental disaster, and not just heading toward it, but *rushing* toward it. The US is in the lead of accelerating these dangers under the pressure of business for in large part institutional reasons. Just take a look at the headlines. There was a report on the front page of the *New York Times*, a revealing report on the measurements of the Arctic ice cap. Well, it turns out the melting was far beyond anything that had been predicted by sophisticated computer models, and the melting of the Arctic ice cap has very substantial effects on the climate altogether.

It's an escalating process because as the ice cap melts, less of the sun's energy is reflected, and more comes into the atmosphere, creating an escalating, nonlinear process that gets out of control. The article also reported the reactions of governments and corporations. Their reaction is enthusiasm. We can now accelerate the process because new areas are open for digging and extraction of fossil fuels, so we can make it worse. That's great.

This is a death sentence for our descendants. Fine, let's accelerate it—hundreds of millions of people in Bangladesh are gonna be driven from their homes by rising sea level in the not-distant future, with consequences for the rest of us too. This demonstrates either a remarkable lack of concern for our own grandchildren and others like them, or else an equally remarkable inability to see what's before our own eyes.

There's another major threat to survival that's been hanging over human life for more than seventy years—and that's nuclear war. And that's increasing. Bertrand Russell and Albert Einstein, around 1955, issued a passionate plea to the people of the world to recognize that they have a choice that is stark and unavoidable: they must decide—all of mankind must decide—to renounce war, or to self-destruct. And we have come very close to self-destruction a number of times. The Bulletin of Atomic Scientists has what it calls a "Dooms-day Clock." It started in 1947, right after the atom bomb was used. The clock measures the distance that we are from midnight—midnight means termination. Just two years ago the clock was moved two minutes closer to midnight—to three minutes before midnight. The reason is that the threat of nuclear war and the threat of environmental catastrophe are increasing. Policy makers are amplifying them, that's the future that we're not only creating but accelerating.

STRUCTURES OF AUTHORITY ARE NOT SELF-JUSTIFYING

I don't think we're smart enough to design in any detail what a perfectly just and free society would be like. I think we can give some guidelines and, more signifi-cantly, we can ask how we can progress in that direction. John Dewey, the leading social philosopher in the late twentieth century, argued that until all institutions—production, commerce, media—are under participatory democratic control, we will not have a functioning demo-cratic society. As he put it, "Policy will be the shadow cast by business over society." Well, it's essentially true.

Where there are structures of authority, domination,

See *The Later Works: 1925–1953, Volume 6: 1931–1932*, John Dewey, 1985, on page 153

and hierarchy—somebody gives the orders and somebody takes them—they are not self-justifying. They have to justify themselves. They have a burden of proof to meet. If you take a close look, usually you find they can't justify themselves. If they can't, we ought to be dismantling them—trying to expand the domain of freedom and justice by dismantling that form of illegitimate authority. That's another task for an organized, committed, dedicated population: not just to regulate them, but to ask why they're there. This comes straight out of the libertarian element of the Enlightenment and classical liberal thought. It's also the core principle of anarchism, but that's democracy as well. I don't think they're in opposition in any respect. They're just different ways of looking at the same kind of problem—popular decision making in the hands of people who are concerned with the decisions and their impact. And, in fact, progress over the years—what we all thankfully recognized as progress—has been just that.

CHANGE

To a nontrivial extent, I've also spent a lot of my life in activism. That doesn't show up publicly. I'm not terribly good at it . . . I'm not the greatest organizer. But the reason things change is because lots of people are working all the time. They're working in their communities, in their workplace, or wherever they happen to be—and they're building up the basis for popular movements, which are going to make changes. That's the way everything has ever happened in history.

See *Brandenburg v. Ohio*, Supreme Court of the United States, June 9, 1969, on page 154

See *Edwards v. South Carolina*, Supreme Court of the United States, February 25, 1963, on page 155

See *Times v. Sullivan*, Supreme Court of the United States, March 9, 1964, on page 156

Take, say, freedom of speech, one of the real achievements of American society—we're first in the world in that. It's not truly guaranteed in the Bill of Rights, in the Constitution. Freedom of speech issues began to come to the Supreme Court in the early twentieth century. The major contributions came in the 1960s. One of the leading ones was a case in the civil rights movement. By then you had a mass popular movement, which was demanding rights, refusing to back down. In that context, the Supreme Court did establish a pretty high standard for freedom of speech. Or take, say, women's rights. Women also began identifying oppressive structures, refusing to accept them, bringing other people to join with them. That's how rights are won.

There is no general remedy. There are particular remedies for particular problems, but there's no general remedy—at least that I know of—for everything. The activists are the people who have created the rights that we enjoy. They're not only carrying out policies based on information that they're receiving, but also contributing to the understanding. Remember, it's a reciprocal process. You try to do things. You learn. You learn about what the world is like. That feeds back to the understanding of how to go on.

The way people learn is by interaction. That's even true of the advanced sciences. If you go to a research lab in the sciences, people are talking to each other, they're challenging each other, they're presenting ideas, getting reactions from colleagues, students, and so on. If you're isolated, you might be an individual genius who can figure things out, but it's not likely. You don't have the resources, or the support, or the encouragement to try to find out who you are, what's happening in the world, where you should be looking, and so on.

So in societies with functioning, significant organizations like labor unions—which were a very educational force, not just fighting for workers' rights, but where workers' education was a major phenomenon—you can learn where to look. You can encourage each other. You can inform each other. You can have your views challenged, refine them, and so on. Then, you can overcome the very natural efforts of elite institutions to protect you from what they don't want you to know. So it's like everything else, a constant struggle against power.

During the Arab Spring, in the early days of the Tahrir Square demonstrations, government pressures were very significant. A lot of the organizing was done through social media, and President Mubarak made the decision to shut down the Internet to block the activism through social media. What was the effect? Activism *increased* because people returned to what really matters, which is face-to-face contact. People began to *talk* to one another. We have plenty of evidence that direct personal interchange—organizing with people directly, talking to them, listening to them, and so on—has a major effect. Social media are useful, and all organizers and activists use them, but it's not like really entering into a discussion with people directly. We're human beings, we're not robots, and I think that can't be forgotten.

So, to the question "what can we do?" Just about anything we choose to do. The fact of the matter is, by comparative standards, we live in quite a free society. It wasn't a gift from heaven. The freedoms that we have were won by hard, painful, courageous popular struggle, but they're there. We have that legacy—a legacy granted to us by the struggles of others. There are huge opportunities—it's still the freest society in the world in many ways. Government has very limited capacity to coerce. Corporate business may try to coerce, but they don't have the mechanisms. There's a lot that can be done if people organize—struggle for their rights as they've done in the past—and we can win many victories.

I think that we can see quite clearly some very, very serious defects and flaws in our society, our level of culture, our institutions—which are going to have to be corrected by operating outside of the framework that is commonly accepted. I think we're going to have to find new ways of political action. There is a change going on, mainly among young people, but that is where change usually starts. Where's it gonna go? That's really up to you. It goes where people like you will direct it.

My close friend for many years, the late Howard Zinn, to put it in his words, said that "what matters is the countless small deeds of unknown people, who lay the basis for the significant events that enter history." They're the ones who've done things in the past. They're the ones who'll have to do it in the future.

See *You Can't Be Neutral on a Moving Train: A Personal History of Our Times,* Howard Zinn, 1994, on page 157

"TESTING THEORIES OF AMERICAN POLITICS," 2014, AND OTHER SOURCES

"Testing Theories of American Politics: Elites, Interest Groups, and Average Citizens," Martin Gilens and Benjamin I. Page, 2014

A great deal of empirical research speaks to the policy influence of one or another set of actors, but until recently it has not been possible to test these contrasting theoretical predictions against each other within a single statistical model. We report on an effort to do so, using a unique data set that includes measures of the key variables for 1,779 policy issues.

Multivariate analysis indicates that economic elites and organized groups representing business interests have substantial independent impacts on U.S. government policy, while average citizens and mass-based interest groups have little or no independent influence. The results provide substantial support for theories of Economic-Elite Domination and for theories of Biased Pluralism, but not for theories of Majoritarian Electoral Democracy or Majoritarian Pluralism . . .

A final point: Even in a bivariate, descriptive sense, our evidence indicates that the responsiveness of the U.S. political system when the general public wants government *action* is severely limited. Because of the impediments to majority rule that were deliberately built into the U.S. political system—federalism, separation of powers, bicameralism—together with further impediments due to anti-majoritarian congressional rules and procedures, the system has a substantial status quo bias. Thus when popular majorities favor the status quo, opposing a given policy change, they are likely to get their way; but when a majority—even a very large majority—of the public favors change, it is not likely to get what it wants. In our 1,779 policy cases, narrow pro-change majorities of the public got the policy changes they wanted only about 30 percent of the time. More strikingly, even overwhelmingly large pro-change majorities, with 80 percent of the public favoring a policy change, got that change only about 43 percent of the time.

In any case, normative advocates of populistic democracy may not be enthusiastic about democracy by coincidence, in which ordinary citizens get what they want from government only when they happen to agree with elites or interest groups that are really calling the shots. When push comes to shove, actual influence matters.

The Later Works: 1925–1953, *Volume 6: 1931–1932,* John Dewey, 1985

I have ventured to quote scattered statements at considerable length because the picture of the immediate situation in Washington is typical. The condition at Washington reflects accurately the condition of politics throughout the country. The former has nothing to do with the realities of American life because the latter is completely out of connection. The situation explains the discontent and disgust of the people with the old parties and it constitutes the opportunity for a new party. We have long been told that politics is unimportant, that government is merely a drag and an interference; that the captains of industry and finance are the wise ones, the leaders in whose hands the fortunes of the country are safely entrusted.

The persons who keep reiterating such sayings forget, or they try to conceal from view, that the confusion, the perplexity, the triviality, the irrelevance, of politics at Washington merely reflect the bankruptcy of industrial "leadership," just as politics in general is an echo, except when it is an accomplice, of the interests of big business. The deadlocks and the impotence of Congress are definitely the mirror of the demonstrated incapacity of the captains of industry and finance to conduct the affairs of the country prosperously as an incident to the process of feathering their own nests. It would be ludicrous, were it not tragic, to believe that an appeal to the unregulated activities of those who have got us into the present crisis will get us out of it, provided they are relieved from the incubus of political action. The magic of eating a hair of the dog which bit you in order to cure hydrophobia is as nothing to the magic involved in the belief that those who have privilege and power will remedy the breakdown they have created. As long as politics is the shadow cast on society by big business, the attenuation of the shadow will not change the substance. The only remedy is new political action based on social interests and realities.

Brandenburg v. Ohio, Supreme Court of the United States, June 9, 1969

Appellant, a Ku Klux Klan leader, was convicted under the Ohio Criminal Syndicalism statute for "advocat[ing] . . . the duty, necessity, or propriety of crime, sabotage, violence, or unlawful methods of terrorism as a means of accomplishing industrial or political reform" and for "voluntarily assembl[ing] with any society, group or assemblage of persons formed to teach or advocate the doctrines of criminal syndicalism."

Neither the indictment nor the trial judge's instructions refined the statute's definition of the crime in terms of mere advocacy not distinguished from incitement to imminent lawless action.

Held: Since the statute, by its words and as applied, purports to punish mere advocacy and to forbid, on pain of criminal punishment, assembly with others merely to advocate the described type of action, it falls within the condemnation of the First and Fourteenth Amendments. Freedoms of speech and press do not permit a State to forbid advocacy of the use of force or of law violation except where such advocacy is directed to inciting or producing imminent lawless action and is likely to incite or produce such action. *Whitney v. California*, 274 U.S. 357, overruled.

Edwards v. South Carolina, Supreme Court of the United States, February 25, 1963

[A] function of free speech under our system of government is to invite dispute. It may indeed best serve its high purpose when it induces a condition of unrest, creates dissatisfaction with conditions as they are, or even stirs people to anger. Speech is often provocative and challenging. It may strike at prejudices and preconceptions, and have profound unsettling effects as it presses for acceptance of an idea. That is why freedom of speech . . . is . . . protected against censorship or punishment, unless shown likely to produce a clear and present danger of a serious substantive evil that rises far above public inconvenience, annoyance, or unrest . . . There is no room under our Constitution for a more restrictive view. For the alternative would lead to standardization of ideas either by legislatures, courts, or dominant political or community groups.

Times v. Sullivan, Supreme Court of the United States, March 9, 1964

Respondent, an elected official in Montgomery, Alabama, brought suit in a state court alleging that he had been libeled by an advertisement in corporate petitioner's newspaper, the text of which appeared over the names of the four individual petitioners and many others. The advertisement included statements, some of which were false, about police action allegedly directed against students who participated in a civil rights demonstration and against a leader of the civil rights movement; respondent claimed the statements referred to him because his duties included supervision of the police department. The trial judge instructed the jury that such statements were "libelous *per se*," legal injury being implied without proof of actual damages, and that, for the purpose of compensatory damages, malice was presumed, so that such damages could be awarded against petitioners if the statements were found to have been published by them and to have related to respondent. As to punitive damages, the judge instructed that mere negligence was not evidence of actual malice, and would not justify an award of punitive damages; he refused to instruct that actual intent to harm or recklessness had to be found before punitive damages could be awarded, or that a verdict for respondent should differentiate between compensatory and punitive damages. The jury found for respondent, and the State Supreme Court affirmed.

Held: A State cannot, under the First and Fourteenth Amendments, award damages to a public official for defamatory falsehood relating to his official conduct unless he proves "actual malice"—that the statement was made with knowledge of its falsity or with reckless disregard of whether it was true or false.

You Can't Be Neutral on a Moving Train: A Personal History of Our Times, Howard Zinn, 1994

The history of social movements often confines itself to the large events, the pivotal moments. Typically, a survey of the history of the civil rights movement will deal with the Supreme Court decision in the Brown case, the Montgomery bus boycott, the sit-ins, the Freedom Rides, the Birmingham demonstrations, the March on Washington, the Civil Rights Act of 1964, the March from Selma to Montgomery, the Voting Rights Act of 1965.

Missing from such histories are the countless small actions of unknown people that led up to those great moments. When we understand this, we can see that the tiniest acts of protest in which we engage may become the invisible roots of social change.

Notes to Primary Source Material

PRINCIPLE #1: REDUCE DEMOCRACY

Yates, Robert, and John Lansing. *Secret Proceedings and Debates of the Convention Assembled at Philadelphia, in the Year 1787*. Cincinnati: A. Mygatt, 1844. https://archive.org/details/secretproceedinooconvgoog.

"From Thomas Jefferson to William Short, 8 January 1825." Founders Online. Last modified October 5, 2016. http://founders.archives.gov/documents/Jefferson/98-01-02-4848.

Martin, Thomas R., with Neel Smith and Jennifer F. Stuart. "Democracy in the Politics of Aristotle." In *Dēmos: Classical Athenian Democracy*, edited by C. W. Blackwell (Anne Mahoney and Ross Scaife, eds., *The Stoa: A Consortium for Electronic Publication in the Humanities* [www.stoa.org]). Last modified July 26, 2003. Accessed November 16, 2016. http://www.stoa.org/projects/demos/article_aristotle_democracy?page=8&greekEncoding.

Aristotle. *Politics*. Edited by R. F. Stalley. Translated by Sir Ernest Barker. Oxford: Oxford University Press, 2009.

Somerset v. Stewart, (1772) 98 E.R. 499 (K.B.).

Malcolm X. "'Democracy is Hypocrisy' speech." Alexander Street video, 6:00. Accessed November 15, 2016. http://search.alexanderstreet.com/preview/work/2787244. Reprinted by permission of the Estate of Malcolm X.

King, Martin Luther, Jr. *A Testament of Hope: The Essential Writings and Speeches of Martin Luther King, Jr.* Edited by James M. Washington. San Francisco: Harper & Row, 1986. Copyright © 1986 by Coretta Scott King, Executrix of the Estate of Martin Luther King, Jr. Reprinted by arrangement with The Heirs to the Estate of Martin Luther King, Jr., c/o Writers House as agent for the proprietor New York, NY.

Nelson, Gaylord. Speeches and other documents on Earth Day, 1970. Gaylord Nelson Papers, MSS 1020. Wisconsin Historical Society. http://www.wisconsinhistory.org/turningpoints/search.asp?id=1671.

PRINCIPLE #2: SHAPE IDEOLOGY

Powell, Lewis Franklin, Jr. *Confidential Memorandum: Attack on American Free Enterprise System (Powell Memorandum).* Washington, DC: 1971. http://reclaimdemocracy.org/powell_memo_lewis/.

Crozier, Michel J., Samuel P. Huntington, and Joji Watanuki. *The Crisis of Democracy: Report on the Governability of Democracies to the Trilateral Commission.* New York: New York University Press, 1975.

Schwarz, Alan. "Attention Disorder or Not, Pills to Help in School." *New York Times*, October 9, 2012. http://www.nytimes.com/2012/10/09/health/attention-disorder-or-not-children-prescribed-pills-to-help-in-school.html. Reprinted by permission of the New York Times.

PRINCIPLE #3: REDESIGN THE ECONOMY

Lahart, Justin. "An End to the Focus on Short Term Urged." *Wall Street Journal*, September 9, 2009. http://www.wsj.com/articles/SB125244043531193463. Copyright © 2009, Dow Jones & Company. Reprinted by permission.

Smith, Adam. *An Inquiry into the Nature and Causes of the Wealth of Nations.* London: W. Strahan and T. Cadell, 1776. http://www.ifaarchive.com/pdf/smith_-_

an_inquiry_into_the_nature_and_causes_of_the_wealth_of_
nations%5B1%5D.pdf.

Bank for International Settlements. *Mr. Greenspan Presents the
Views of the Federal Reserve in Its Semi-annual Report on
Monetary Policy, February 26, 1997.* Accessed November 10,
2016. http://www.bis.org/review/r970305b.pdf.

PRINCIPLE #4: SHIFT THE BURDEN

Nilsson, Jeff. "Why Did Henry Ford Double His Minimum
Wage?" *Saturday Evening Post*, January 3, 2014. http://www.
saturdayeveningpost.com/2014/01/03/history/post-perspec-
tive/ford-doubles-minimum-wage.html.

Terrell, Ellen. "When a Quote Is Not (Exactly) a Quote: General
Motors." *Inside Adams* (blog), Library of Congress, April 22,
2016. https://blogs.loc.gov/inside_adams/2016/04/when-a-
quote-is-not-exactly-a-quote-general-motors/.

Citigroup. *Plutonomy: Buying Luxury, Explaining Global Imbalances.* New York: 2005. https://docs.google.com/file/d/0B-
5-JeCa2Z7hNWQyN2l1YjYtZTJjNy00ZWU3LWEwNDEt-
MGVhZDVjNzEwZDZm/edit?hl=en_US.

Standard & Poor's. *Economic Research: How Increasing In-
come Inequality Is Dampening U.S. Economic Growth, and
Possible Ways to Change the Tide.* New York: 2014. http://
www.ncsl.org/Portals/1/Documents/forum/Forum_2014/
Income_Inequality.pdf. Copyright © 2014 Standard & Poor's
Financial Services LLC. Reprinted by permission.

PRINCIPLE #5: ATTACK SOLIDARITY

Smith, Adam. *The Theory of Moral Sentiments.* London: A. Mil-
lar, 1759. http://www.econlib.org/library/Smith/smMS1.html.

Social Security Act of 1935, Pub. L. No. 74-271, 49 Stat. 620 (1935).

Servicemen's Readjustment Act of 1944, Pub. L. No. 78-346, 58
Stat. 284 (1944).

PRINCIPLE #6: RUN THE REGULATORS

Hacker, Jacob S., and Nate Loewentheil. *Prosperity Economics: Building an Economy for All*. Creative Commons, 2012. Accessed November 9, 2016. http://isps.yale.edu/sites/default/files/publication/2013/01/2012-prosperity-for-all.pdf. Reprinted (Creative Commons, 2012), 18, 29.

Drutman, Lee. "How Corporate Lobbyists Conquered American Democracy." *New America Weekly*, New America, April 20, 2015. http://www.newamerica.org/political-reform/articles/how-corporate-lobbyists-conquered-american-democracy/. Reprinted courtesy of New America Weekly, New America.

Ruigrok, Winfried, and Rob van Tulder. *The Logic of International Restructuring: The Management of Dependencies in Rival Industrial Complexes*. Abingdon, UK: Routledge, 1995. Copyright © 1995 Winfried Ruigrok and Rob van Tulder. Reprinted by permission.

Smith, Adam. *An Inquiry into the Nature and Causes of the Wealth of Nations*. London: W. Strahan and T. Cadell, 1776. http://www.ifaarchive.com/pdf/smith_-_an_inquiry_into_the_nature_and_causes_of_the_wealth_of_nations%5B1%5D.pdf.

Irelan, John Robert. *The Republic, Or, A History of the United States of America in the Administrations: From the Monarchic Colonial Days to the Present Times, Volume 10*. Chicago: Fairbanks and Palmer Publishing Company, 1888.

PRINCIPLE #7: ENGINEER ELECTIONS

Citizens United v. Federal Election Commission, 558 U.S. 310 (2010).

Buckley v. Valeo, 424 U.S. 1 (1976).

Ferguson, Thomas, Paul Jorgensen, and Jie Chen. "Revealed: Why the Pundits Are Wrong About Big Money and the 2012 Elections." AlterNet, December 20, 2012. http://www.alternet.org/news-amp-politics/revealed-why-pundits-are-wrong-about-big-money-and-2012-elections. Reprinted by permission of AlterNet.

PRINCIPLE #8: KEEP THE RABBLE IN LINE

"Ford Men Beat and Rout Lewis Union Organizers; 80,000 Out in Steel Strike; 16 Hurt in Battle." *New York Times*, May 26, 1937. http://query.nytimes.com/mem/archive-free/pdf?res=9 A02E2DF1E3AE23ABC4F51DFB366838C629EDE.

Truman, Harry S. "Address in Louisville, Kentucky, September 30, 1948." In *Public Papers of the Presidents of the United States: Harry S. Truman, 1948*. Citation online by Gerhard Peters and John T. Woolley, American Presidency Project. http://www.presidency.ucsb.edu/ws/?pid=13029.

"Douglas Fraser's Resignation Letter from the Labor-Management Group." History is a Weapon. Accessed November 9, 2016. http://www.historyisaweapon.com/defcon1/fraserresign.html.

Hedges, Chris. "Power Concedes Nothing Without a Demand." *Truthdig*, March 14, 2011. http://www.truthdig.com/report/ item/power_concedes_nothing_without_a_demand_20110314.

PRINCIPLE #9: MANUFACTURE CONSENT

Hume, David. *Essays, Moral, Political, Literary*. London: Kincaid, 1741. http://www.econlib.org/library/LFBooks/Hume/hmMPL4.html.

Bernays, Edward. *Propaganda*. New York: H. Liveright, 1928.

Amos, Amanda, and Margaretha Haglund. "From Social Taboo to 'Torch of Freedom': The Marketing of Cigarettes to Women." *Tobacco Control* 9 no. 1 (2000): 3–8.

Schlosser, Eric. *Fast Food Nation: The Dark Side of the All-American Meal*. New York: Houghton Mifflin, 2001. Copyright © 2001 by Eric Schlosser. Reprinted by permission of Houghton Mifflin Harcourt Publishing Company. All rights reserved.

Lichtenstein, Alex. *Twice the Work of Free Labor: The Political Economy of Convict Labor in the New South*. New York: Verso, 1996. Copyright © Alex Lichtenstein 1996. Reprinted by permission.

Creamer, Matthew. "Obama Wins! . . . Ad Age's Marketer of the Year." *Advertising Age*, October 17, 2008. http://adage.com/article/moy-2008/obama-wins-ad-age-s-marketer-year/131810/.

PRINCIPLE #10: MARGINALIZE THE POPULATION

Gilens, Martin, and Benjamin I. Page. "Testing Theories of American Politics: Elites, Interest Groups, and Average Citizens." *Perspectives on Politics* 12, no. 3 (2014): 564–581. Copyright © American Political Science Association 2014. Reprinted by permission.

Dewey, John. *The Later Works of John Dewey, 1925–1953, Volume 6: 1931–1932*. Carbondale, IL: Southern Illinois University Press, 1985. Copyright © 1985, 2008 by the Board of Trustees, Southern Illinois University. Reprinted courtesy of Southern Illinois University Press.

Edwards v. South Carolina, 372 U.S. 229 (1963).

Brandenburg v. Ohio, 395 U.S. 444 (1969).

New York Times Co. v. Sullivan, 376 U.S. 254 (1964).

Zinn, Howard. *You Can't Be Neutral on a Moving Train: A Personal History of Our Times*. Boston: Beacon Press, 1994. Copyright © 1994, 2002 by Howard Zinn. Reprinted by permission.

Index

About the Author

Political philosopher, activist, and linguist **NOAM CHOMSKY** is beloved around the world for the strength of his personal commitment to the truth as he sees it and for the brilliance of his ideas. Born in Philadelphia on December 7, 1928, he studied linguistics, mathematics, and philosophy at the University of Pennsylvania and received his PhD there in 1955. Chomsky has taught at MIT for fifty years and is currently Institute Professor Emeritus in the Department of Linguistics and Philosophy. His linguistics work is widely credited with having revolutionized the field, and his political writings have made important contributions for decades. In 2001, he published *9-11*, which became his first international bestseller and was arguably the single most influential post–9-11 book. Chomsky is the author of many other best-selling political works, including *Profit Over People*, *Media Control*, *Hegemony or Survival*, *Failed States*, *Hopes and Prospects*, *Masters of Mankind*, *What Kind of Creatures Are We?*, and *Who Rules the World?*

About the Editors

PETER HUTCHISON is an NYC-based filmmaker, educator, and activist. His documentary work includes *What Would Jesus Buy?* with producing partner Morgan Spurlock; *Split: A Divided America*; *Beyond Activism: Four Decades of Social Justice*; and *Awake Zion: Rasta, Reggae & Judaism*.

KELLY NYKS is an award-winning writer/director of documentary films and has worked across Europe, Asia, and America. His prior films include *The Age of Consequences*, *Disobedience*, *Disruption*, *Do the Math*, *Split: A Divided America*, and *Split: A Deeper Divide*.

Award-winning writer, director, and producer **JARED P. SCOTT**'s other films include *The Age of Consequences*, *Disruption*, *Do the Math*, and *The Artificial Leaf.* His films have screened at Tribeca, Hot Docs, Sheffield, and IDFA, and have aired/streamed on Netflix, Starz, PBS, and Al Jazeera.

About Seven Stories Press

SEVEN STORIES PRESS is an independent book publisher based in New York City. We publish works of the imagination by such writers as Nelson Algren, Russell Banks, Octavia E. Butler, Ani DiFranco, Assia Djebar, Ariel Dorfman, Coco Fusco, Barry Gifford, Martha Long, Luis Negrón, Hwang Sok-yong, Lee Stringer, and Kurt Vonnegut, to name a few, together with political titles by voices of conscience, including Subhankar Banerjee, the Boston Women's Health Collective, Noam Chomsky, Angela Y. Davis, Human Rights Watch, Derrick Jensen, Ralph Nader, Loretta Napoleoni, Gary Null, Greg Palast, Project Censored, Barbara Seaman, Alice Walker, Gary Webb, and Howard Zinn, among many others. Seven Stories Press believes publishers have a special responsibility to defend free speech and human rights, and to celebrate the gifts of the human imagination, wherever we can. In 2012 we launched Triangle Square books for young readers with strong social justice and narrative components, telling personal stories of courage and commitment. For additional information, visit www.sevenstories.com.